D0442786

12
NOTES

On Life and Creativity

QUINCY
JONES

Foreword by The Weeknd

Abrams Image, New York

Co-Author: Alyssa Lein Smith
Editor: Rebecca Kaplan
Editorial Consultant: Ben Fong-Torres
Designer: Diane Shaw
Design Manager: Jenice Kim
Managing Editor: Annalea Manalili
Production Manager: Sarah Masterson Hally

Library of Congress Control Number: 2021932496

ISBN: 978-1-4197-5256-8
eISBN: 978-1-64700-208-4

Printed and bound in the United States
10 9 8 7 6 5 4 3 2 1

Abrams Image books are available at special discounts when purchased in quantity for premiums and promotions as well as fundraising or educational use. Special editions can also be created to specification. For details, contact specialsales@abramsbooks.com or the address below.

Abrams Image® is a registered trademark of Harry N. Abrams, Inc.

ABRAMS The Art of Books
195 Broadway, New York, NY 10007
abramsbooks.com

DEDICATED TO MY SEVEN
BELOVED AND CHERISHED RUGRATS:
JOLIE, RACHEL, TINA, QDIII,
KIDADA, RASHIDA & KENYA

FOREWORD

I'm just going to start off by saying that there are *no* words to accurately describe the man who is Quincy Jones: The man who changed not only the course of my life, but the course of history. I'm not here to tell you about the awards, accolades, and accomplishments that Quincy has received or achieved, because (1) we'd be here all day; and (2) we already know he *is that* dude. No qualifiers necessary. However, I will share how the work that he does when the cameras are off has often been the most impactful.

Allow me to explain. I had of course been a huge fan of Q's since I was a kid, and the music he made with Michael Jackson inspired me to pursue music even more. Q was my idol in every sense of the word and I tried to soak up any clues to greatness he may have left behind. I felt as though I knew him, because I practically did know everything about him and his work, but we hadn't yet met in person.

Fast forward to 2015, when Victor Drai surprised me by bringing Q to my show at Drai's Nightclub in Las Vegas. I nearly lost my mind after I heard that my idol was sitting on the side of the stage, about to watch me perform. As soon as I finished my last song, I couldn't make it over to him fast enough. I was so laser-focused on meeting him (the reason why I even do music in the first place) that I barely even noticed there were fans on the other side of the stage, screaming my name, trying to grab my attention.

The first thing Q told me as I approached him was, "Go to your fans. Take pictures and sign autographs with them. I'll still be here waiting for you afterward. They're more important."

Out of all the lessons I learned from watching his public interviews or listening to his productions for hours on end, that one piece of instruction proved to be more meaningful. At that moment, he was teaching me something that I will never forget. Nothing is more valuable than the people around me, and giving back is *always* better than receiving.

I did as I was told, and after I finished meeting with the fans, Q (the legend of all legends) was still there, waiting. His humility was beyond me. In this business, it's common to think you're the biggest VIP on earth, after earning a hit record and a bit of fame. But to see the man who has achieved more than anyone else carry himself without a single ounce of selfishness was the best example of walking the talk.

Fast forward once more to September 2021, when I received the inaugural Quincy Jones Humanitarian Award at the Music in Action Awards hosted by the Black Music Action Coalition. To say this was an honor is an understatement, but when my words fail me, I let my music speak, so maybe one day you'll get to hear about it.

I received a lot of props on the heels of this achievement, but as Q taught me through his words and actions, giving back isn't something to be praised. It is something to be done, regardless of recognition.

The small, private moments are often what matter most, and if anything, this book is about that exact dynamic. It means a lot to me because although I have a public persona, I tend to be a very private person. I'm still the same Ethiopian kid from

Toronto who grew up without a father. And Q is still the same kid from Chicago who grew up without a mother. We may have different, personal reasons for creating, but I know we'll never forget where we came from, and why giving back is always more important than receiving.

As Q so beautifully says in the final chapter of this book: "My hope and prayer is that our individual, creative voices may serve to share a glimpse of connectivity with those who need it most." And I can only hope that is what my art has done and will continue to do.

We've all made mistakes—myself included—but that's why I love Q. He isn't afraid to confront them head on and use them as fuel to become a better person. This book is no exception. If anything, it's about to become the rule.

On June 14, 2015, I tweeted, "Quincy Jones came last night to watch me perform and I'm still trying to process it."

On September 23, 2021, I accepted the Quincy Jones Humanitarian Award—the best award I've ever gotten in my life.

And today, I write the foreword to *12 Notes: On Life and Creativity*. It's an honor I will never take for granted, so Q, thank you. Thank you for everything you've taught me publicly, and everything you've taught me through your words and actions.

To everyone else reading this: Even if you've already read his autobiography or know everything there is to know about him, I hope you'll take time to listen to the advice he has to share with you in the pages of this book. Because I promise it is what matters the most.

—Abel "The Weeknd" Tesfaye

INTRODUCTION

I'm often asked what my "formula for success" is, or what my road map is to becoming (at the time of this writing) the all-time most Grammy®–nominated artist, but to be honest, there is no formula or road map, and if anyone tells you there is, they're full of it. But, I like to think that this book is the closest I will get to sharing my personal "formula." I'm not here to tell you how to live, or what to do for a living, but I want to share the lessons I've learned, the advice I've received, and the conclusions I've come to about life and creativity that have allowed me to live an enriched life, full of highs and lows. A life of purpose.

My hope for this book is that anyone at any age can relate to the stories I'm about to share. I was in a much different place when I wrote and published my autobiography in 2001, and it was an entirely different kind of project. That book was a way for me to share chapters of my life.

12 Notes: On Life and Creativity is a book meant to elevate and transform your mind, through the sharing of advice and techniques I've learned throughout my time here on this planet. The beauty of looking back on my life, after I've had the privilege of living a good chunk of it, is that I can see everything so clearly: the distractions and the transformations. After I quit drinking alcohol in 2015, all my memories came flooding back, and they brought new perspectives with them that I've now been able to distill into crucial pieces of advice that I want to share with anyone looking to break through the walls that often withhold creativity.

I write this book for the young artist who might be finding himself or herself in the shoes that I was once in, trying to navigate a unique path in the industry. But, I also write this book for those who have lived their entire lives under the guise of a career or lifestyle that they never truly wanted. Much to our collective disadvantage, the rules of society have led many to believe that creativity is only valuable for the artists who make a name for themselves. I call bs because we ALL have creative potential and we all deserve to realize it; it's only a matter of whether or not we allow ourselves to fulfill it.

Now, to provide you with a bit of background about the organizational structure of the book, the number twelve has always had a special meaning in my life. Nadia Boulanger, my former teacher in Paris, used to tell me, "Quincy, there are only twelve notes. Until God gives us thirteen, I want you to know what everybody did with those twelve." Bach, Beethoven, Bo Diddley, everybody . . . it's the same twelve notes. Isn't it amazing? That's all we have, and it's up to each of us to create our own unique sound through a combination of rhythm, harmony, and melody.

I'm always fascinated to hear the different outcomes that we as musicians can create with only twelve notes; in the same way, I want to break down my principles, my approach to life, and my philosophies, along with standout stories from my journey (people like to call me "Forrest Gump," but you know, I prefer "Ghetto Gump"), in twelve chapters (or in the case of this book, I'll be calling them "notes"). So, feel free to skip around, mix and match, take what you want, and leave what you don't. No matter what, I know the outcome will be b-e-a-utiful. The staff paper is yours and it's up to you to do what you want with it. Big-time love and props!

—Quincy Jones

PURPOSE

When we really break it down, creativity is made up of two parts: science and soul (left and right brain). The scientific side is that which needs to be learned and practiced. But the soulful side (which is composed of emotions) is something that can't be taught—it's simply the essence of who you are as a human being. Well, the essence of who I am has been wrapped in so much trauma, that it was forced to find a way out, with creative expression as its method of escape. Growing up in an environment that stripped me of all ability to control my circumstances, creativity became the only way in which I could gain even an ounce of stability.

After my family moved to the Pacific Northwest, I would mentally transport myself to an imaginary world filled with music whenever anything bad happened to me. It was my escape when I simply couldn't handle what was going on in my life. And, I guess in many ways, I've been crawling into that same world for a very long time, converting my negative energy into creativity. It allows me to express my emotions when I am suppressed, and gives me the permission to share what I otherwise would not be able to convey with words alone.

For example, when I think about my late brother Marvin Gaye's revolutionary 1971 single "What's Going On," I can't help but consider all of his personal experiences that informed the track—from loss, to social and political unrest, to war and racial tensions. Nobody really knew what was going on at the time, but he and his fellow songwriters channeled their questions, pain, and collective feeling of confusion into that song, both lyrically and sonically. Despite the hostile environment and tragic stories that gave way to his creativity, he was able to mold his hurt into healing—healing for those who needed words of hope or a sign of mutual understanding about the state of the world.

As I write, it's evident that we're still dealing with similar emotions and marching to some of the very same lyrics. There's no doubt it is an incredibly powerful piece of music that has become a universal anthem for millions of people, even long after Marvin's tragic death. Man, I miss him.

We all have different methods of expression, and although it may not sound or look exactly like anthems such as "What's Going On," "We Are the World," or "Let It Be," we have the ability to channel our life experiences into something greater than ourselves. In the midst of adversity, it's easy to let disappointment or anger take center stage, but I have found that my purpose is so much greater than my problems, although it's incredibly easy to place an emphasis on the latter.

I've had my fair share of ups and downs throughout my more than eighty-eight years on this planet (who you callin' elderly?), but the most beautiful part about this age is being able to look back on each stage of life and see the visible threads that held it all together, when at times I could've sworn everything was falling apart. Music not only became one of those threads, but it assumed a very important role in my life. You see, I didn't have a mother in the traditional sense, so in a way, I made *music* my mother.

As a warning, the story behind how I learned the importance of recycling my pain into purpose might be a bit difficult to digest, but telling you the details is really the only way to explain how I've been able to translate my negativity into creativity.

1942. Age 9.

"We're going to see your mama," Daddy said.

Mama. A four-letter word that was not only devoid of personal connection, but warranted a rent-free occupancy for fear to live in my head. I didn't know exactly where my daddy was driving us, but myself and my little brother, Lloyd, who sat next to me in the backseat of my father's old struggle-buggy Buick, were powerless as we forged ahead. After driving for what seemed like endless rotations on the clock, we finally arrived at the scene: a row of towering white brick buildings, juxtaposed with a surrounding backdrop of green grass, flowers, and trees. As Lloyd and I stepped out of the car, I caught a glimpse of a sign that read "Manteno State Hospital."

The long sidewalk leading up to the entrance became like quicksand beneath my feet, with every step more difficult than the last. The ominous glow of light reflecting off the unbearably white building was soon to envelop us and light our path until we reached our destination. The daunting double wooden doors that separated the inside from the rest of the world seemed to mock us as we slowly, yet curiously, stepped inside.

An immediate wave of Lysol fragrances filled my nostrils in a futile attempt to mask the vile stench of urine and sweat. I wanted to turn back, but it was too late. My fear turned into disbelief as I tried to convince myself that what I was witnessing in the halls wasn't real: human beings dressed in identical gowns sprawled across the floors and on top of furniture in a haphazard manner. Some lying down, some screaming, some curled into balls in the corner, others laughing hysterically to themselves, and the majority moving about the room like the walking dead.

Without warning, it was as if they all stopped and noticed us in unison; the energy shifted, and from out of the corner, a barefoot woman burst through the group and darted toward us. My already-existing posture of distress was heightened as she frantically screamed, "You shall have no pie! You shall have no pie!" She held out a bowl full of what turned out to be human feces. Daddy blocked us from the immediate threat, and quickly pushed us down to the end of the hall. His grasp on our shoulders seemed a likely intent to comfort, but it only increased my anxiety as I could feel that the hands of our protector were trembling.

Finally, after making our way through what felt like a sea of lost souls, our eyes were met with the most terrifying reflection of ourselves. My mother. Sarah. Her frail body was clothed in a hospital gown, identical to that of her peers, and her feet barely fit into a pair of battered slippers. Daddy firmly called out to her, and she peered up at us as she seemed to slowly register who she was seeing. A slight smile brightened up her dimly lit face, and reminded me of the smile I used to receive as a five-year-old, after she had combed my hair, washed my face, and helped me put on my clothes. It lasted but a minute, then the hopeful look of recognition was overtaken by an anger that furrowed across her eyebrows.

"Say hello to the boys," my father requested, only to be met with silence. Her muted response gave way to a rant: one conspiracy theory after the other. From a woman she believed my father was "seeing," to Jesus, to Joe Louis, to the Pope. Daddy tried to calm her down, but she shot back with "You took my boys away! I had a life until your gangster priests dragged me off! I can't sleep here!"

"Say hello to the boys, Sarah," he kept telling her. Back and forth they went, until she began to yell louder and louder. As she reached peak volume, her flailing arms froze still, just in time for her to squat down and place her hands underneath as she defecated into one palm, dipped a finger into her newly created product, and raised it to her mouth.

My father wasn't an angry man, but when he lost his temper, he really lost it. He cried out in horror while lurching forward to knock it out of her hand. The force took her down, but she quickly got up and tried to run after us as my father dragged me and Lloyd out by our collars. Her high-pitched screams seemed to follow us as we made it back to our makeshift safety zone, the doors of our Buick that was parked outside.

"I'm so sorry," he kept repeating. "I'm sorry I brought y'all here. To see that. You have to understand. Your mama's not well."

"Your mama's not well." A phrase I heard repeatedly throughout my childhood. A phrase that haunted me. A phrase that would subconsciously inform much of the way I operated in my later years. The crippling fear of developing dementia and becoming as crazy as she was began to set in and fill the crevices of my mind. Night after night, there seemed to be no escape. Even my waking moments were filled with my mother's ever-present voices, enough to convince me that I was, in fact, going crazy. If she could, couldn't I? Or, was I already?

I'm convinced there are two kinds of people: those who have been properly nurtured and those who haven't. There's really nothing in between. When you've been nurtured, you know it, and when you haven't, you really know it. The aftereffects start rearing their ugly head through the ways in which you see and treat others, and maybe even less apparently, the ways in which you see and treat yourself. It starts seeping through the cracks of the drywall you try to put up in your soul, and eventually it begins to leak into your every move, and unfortunately in my case, every REM cycle.

Almost every night since my mother had been taken away to the Manteno State Hospital due to extreme bouts of dementia praecox—roughly two years before our in-person visit—I was afflicted by a very strange nightmare that seemed to pursue me no matter how hard I tried to shake it. Within the walls of this dream, I was sitting at a piano, playing classical music consisting of no identifiable notes or melodies. My mother would then appear behind me, beseeching me to stop playing, and her voice would warp into a mixture of two, then four, then one hundred, then one thousand, all combining to fill my head with her angry exhortations. In each nightmare, as her presence continued to split into multiple figures, I discovered that in order to combat her voices, I had to raise my own.

While still sitting and playing at the piano, I'd muster up enough energy to shout back in response, "Please, stop it! Somebody sing about love. Somebody sing about lovin' me." The more forcefully I declared this, the quicker her instructions would fall silent, and some semblance of sanity would be restored in the midst of another sleepless night.

Little did I know that my response to her demands in my nightmares proved to be indicative of who I would become in the long run. Although I hadn't yet learned to play instruments at that age—I was only ten years old—it was as if the piano in my nightmares served to foreshadow the path that lay before me, and prove that music would be my weapon. I would use it not only to calm the voices in my head, but also to spread the sense of joy that I longed for. In some way, my words reflected a growing desire to be loved and to spread love. The type of love I wanted to see within a family. The type of love I longed for from my mother.

Seeing the woman who was supposed to care for and protect me get tied up and taken to a mental institution is enough to rattle any kid's world, let alone a kid who also lived in the ghetto with no real role models. With no mother and a father who was always away at work, I had no compass, and at times, a pervasive feeling of hopelessness.

Although my suffering and anger were real and valid, I learned the importance of not keeping it locked inside. As Mark Twain poignantly stated, "Anger is an acid that can do more harm to the vessel in which it is stored than to anything on which it is poured." I learned that the hard way, after seeking a sense of safety and belonging, under the purview of gang associations, to later falling into what often turned into unhealthy relationships, to workaholism, to you name it. Don't worry, we'll get there later on.

But despite the holes and negative experiences from my upbringing, I know I'm one of the lucky ones. Over the course of my lifetime, it has seemed as though God has guided me with an internal feeling that my encounters weren't meant to destroy me. Rather, they were meant to provide me with the empathy I needed to be able to relate to and help others in similar positions, to give me an undeniable drive that has propelled me into arenas of life that I never could've possibly dreamed of, and to generate the deep level of emotion that has been poured into every one of my musical creations. I'm fortunate enough to have figured out that pain has a voice, and music is the method of escape for mine. Now, it feels as though it was always inside of me; I simply had to nurture it and allow it to speak. In a way, I guess that's why so much of the music I've made since then has been about love.

I often wish I could've had a real relationship with my mother, but who knows? Maybe if I had started out with a stable family I would have turned out to be a pitiful musician. As a result of my maternal void, I allowed *music* to assume the role of my mother, and it has been a guiding force in my life ever since. In all honesty, without enduring the level of pain that permeated much of my developmental years, I may have never found my medium of expression and applied myself to it in the manner in which I have.

With the inevitability of hardship in this often broken world, it's important to understand what fills your voids and also where you are projecting yours. The moment you slip into a victim mentality, not only are you faced with having to deal with external problems, but you've also given yourself a whole new set of internal problems that will only stunt your growth as both a human and a creative being. You don't have to let the anguish that has permeated pockets of your life completely take over. I also believe this is why creativity is one of the most beautiful gifts we possess. If utilized properly, not only does it serve as an outlet, but it also holds the power to transform heartache into something beyond a singular sentiment.

Our individual experiences are of course unique to us, but the emotions that we deal with are universal—odds are, someone else can relate. This is why we need creativity. It brings a sense of unity. A painting, a song, a piece of writing—there's power in all of it. Think about why we have archaeology; according to *National Geographic*, the definition of this field of science is "the study of the human past using material remains. These remains can be any objects that people created, modified, or used." When we think about creativity, we often become a bit myopic in our approach, thinking that it's only for ourselves, but it's so much greater. Creativity allows us to leave parts of our experiences and our heart with those on the receiving end. And whether it's now, or long after we've left this planet, I believe there's a reason for it all.

Now, I can't say I learned how to do it all in one day. I know full well that I have had to consistently try to rise above the waves that have threatened to keep me down. But the only way I have even made it to this age is because I chose to learn and grow from my limitations.

It's easy to get tied up in the webs that are woven around us, but then we only close ourselves off to anything new in our lives. Someone once told me that if you fully open your arms to receive love, you'll get some scratches and cuts, but a lot of love will come in. If you close your arms, you might never get cut, but the good stuff will never come to you either.

There's a saying that trauma is frozen at the peak, and if you stay trapped at the top, you'll die. Sometimes mentally, sometimes physically, and sometimes both. And if you close yourself off to the message that you are meant to share, you may never have to face your personal fears and trauma, but nothing good will ever come from it.

Whenever we get hung up and locked into the past, we are completely robbing ourselves of the present, and definitely the future. We can sit in the negativity of the days gone by or we can use it as fuel to propel our creativity, and life, forward. In most cases, extreme mental illness aside, we ultimately have the choice to decide what we focus on: the good or the bad.

Sure, you can hold on to your anger, but bitterness will only destroy you. I've had to make a conscious, daily decision that I wasn't going to destroy myself, but instead I was going to redirect that energy and put it into a song, an arrangement, a record, or a movie—kind of like taking garbage and making recycled paper out of it. It's not easy. But it's possible.

Although it wasn't until I was well into my fifties that I came to realize I was still carrying around my past and allowing it to weigh myself down, I'm glad I got there. It's never too late. When I finally stopped thinking about myself and started thinking about my mother, I thought about all of the horrible things she had gone through in her past, as well as at that hospital, and how much she loved us deep down, even if it was expressed through the lens of her dementia. Although I got to this realization really late in life, I did get to that place, and in the end that's what matters. Life takes unexpected turns, and we may find ourselves in painful situations that we never could have prepared ourselves for. We're all thrown different curveballs, and some may hit harder than others; however, I truly believe that with the proper attitude, the very thing that was intended to destroy you can become the thing that makes you stronger.

You may be angry. These are difficult times and you may have a good reason for feeling that way. But imagine a world where instead of holding on to our anger, we use it to channel a more communal sense of love to make up for the lack thereof. What a world it would be. My hope is that as you continue to read this book, you'll be encouraged to create. Not only for yourself, but for others. Whether you create from a position of pain or jubilation, we need you, your gifts, and your talents. And I say that from experience—more than eighty-eight years of it.

We need you,
your gifts,
and your talents.

IF YOU CAN

SEE IT

YOU CAN

BE IT

NOTE

A#

As I've learned throughout my lifetime, personal growth is just a journey from mind pollution to mind solution. In other words, you have to sift through the dirt of whatever situation it is that you find yourself in, so that your future isn't polluted before you've even had a chance to create it. Whether it's a past trauma or a difficult family situation, mentally overcoming such challenges is often the most important first step in personal advancement.

But, as someone who has dealt with these types of challenges, and more, I recognize that it's easier said than done. In fact, I believe that a great deal of young people who wind up in life-altering trouble have simply been polluted by the supposition that they have no way out, or that their only option is violence. For those born into unfavorable living conditions, or who find themselves without proper support, such a situation can dictate the course of one's life. I believe that our youth *should* have the freedom to grow into their fullest individual potential, but, unfortunately, society has constructed environments that don't always foster equal faith in the future for all. More specifically, cycles of gang violence, drug addiction, and high crime rates in areas of low opportunity are perpetuated in endless circles of hopelessness. It's evident that disadvantaged children are not the victims of some kind of natural disaster, but often, of mankind.

As the saying goes, "You want to be what you see," but if there are no tangible examples of what your life can look like, or attainable ways in which you can achieve that vision, it's incredibly easy to believe that your current position is your only position. Take it from me, I've been there. Having grown up in the South Side of Chicago—the biggest Black ghetto in America during the Great Depression—I didn't exactly come up in an environment that fostered childhood safety, let alone encourage personal drive and ambition. There were no community programs created to spark the mind of a child, and access to other sources of inspirational content was limited, especially before the advent of the internet. I mean, we had books like *See Jane Run* and *See Spot*, but nothing really positive about Black history or anything to anchor our identity.

Despite this, I've noticed that one of the main factors in my ability to outgrow my circumstances was my increased exposure to *hope*, and my relentless pursuit of it. Some may use the word "opportunity" instead, but it's important to note that without hope, opportunities do nothing more than demonstrate to a disadvantaged individual what they are unqualified to be.

How I found slivers of hope in the midst of a hopeless environment is a bit circuitous, but as my beloved brother Louis Armstrong always used to say, "Play it, don't say it." So, let's jump over to 1943 when I really began to learn the true value behind the old adage: "If you can see it you can be it."

When my little brother, Lloyd, and I were kids, my daddy was a carpenter for the Jones Boys, the most notorious Black gangsters in Chicago who ran the numbers game, or what was then called the policy racket (an illegal betting system that later turned into what we now know as the lottery). These guys were the ultimate policy kings, and living under Daddy's roof, with no mother to keep us in check, led to a great deal of exposure to his bosses' rough lifestyle. It was all Lloyd and I ever really knew, and a future as a ganglord or some similar type of character seemed inevitable, as it was surely in my deck of cards. Although Daddy loved us and tried his best to keep us from seeing the Jones Boys' operations on an intimate level, all I wanted was to be like them because they represented what it meant to be in control in an environment that was filled with chaos.

Running across dead bodies, fights that resulted in dead bodies, or other such encounters that ultimately scar the mind of a developing child were pretty much daily occurrences for me.

Speaking of scars, I once had my hand nailed to a fence with a switchblade and an ice pick stabbed into my left temple simply because I didn't have the right password to cross the street. With such conditions, a single ounce of control was all I wanted, and the only thing I saw that would offer it to me was earned under the "protection" of joining a gang. When I say I had to fight to survive, I mean it. The power that I saw behind the curtains of violence was not only what I wanted, but also what I felt I needed in order to survive. There wasn't much to do besides get in trouble, so that's what I did. It wasn't just the normal thing to do, it was expected.

After Al Capone ran the Jones Boys out of town around 1943 for cutting into his profits, my daddy also ran out of town with me and Lloyd for safety's sake. By way of a Trailways bus, we made it to Sinclair Heights in Bremerton, Washington. We may have moved to a new town, but Lloyd and I were still striving to be baby gangsters. We figured that if the Jones Boys and all the gangsters back home ran Chicago, well then, we had our own territory to run now.

But to complicate things even more, we found ourselves in a position with a new, abusive stepmother, Elvera, who was no mother to us at all. As fearful as we were on the inside, our exterior assumed a position of control by bulldozing through anything that got in our way. We imitated what we saw members of the gangs from back home do, and retained the mentality that if you want it, you go out and get it, by any means necessary. Breaking and entering. Stealing and escaping. That was our life, day in and day out. Aside from school, there were no playgrounds, parks, or anything remotely safe to keep us occupied. All we had were miles and miles of evergreen trees in the wilderness and plenty of ways to get into trouble.

Even after landing a job as a paperboy delivering newspapers to the Army base next door to us, I'd always find my way into the ammo dumps and secretly fill my empty newspaper bags with ammo belts, complete naval attire, and live artillery rounds. This was a daily activity, because it at least gave me, Lloyd, and my new stepsiblings (Elvera's kids) a way to stay occupied by dressing up and imitating the cool Black sailors from the segregated Navy base.

Soon enough, I got caught stealing ammo and had to shift my criminal skills elsewhere. More specifically, I decided to target desserts at the local rec center. Lloyd, my new stepbrother Waymond, and I broke in after hearing they had lemon meringue pie and ice cream in the freezer. We ate it all up, had a food fight, then split up to explore the building. I peered into one office and was about to close the door when all I saw was a little spinet piano in the corner. But with unquenchable curiosity, it was as if something deep inside ordered me to "Go back into that room!"

I slowly walked over and ran my fingers across the keys. I'm telling you, it was as if every cell in my body yelled, "This is what you're going to do the rest of your life!" I didn't really understand what that feeling meant, but something about hearing the sound of the piano brought me peace. I didn't know how it worked, or even how to play it, but each note I struck seemed to be paired with an increasing desire to understand how the sound was generated. My brothers caught up with me, and we made our escape from the building unscathed. But, I'd been enraptured, capti-vated by another force. No matter how hard I tried, I couldn't shake the feeling that I needed to get back to that piano.

I longed for the sound of those notes day after day, and I eventually started climbing through the window of the locked rec center to try and play around on the piano. I managed to break in a few more times, until the kind old superintendent, Mrs. Ayres, caught on and began unlocking the door for me. With my newfound access to this magnificent instrument, I tried to mimic the sounds I had heard at the old Baptist Church I attended in Chicago (little did I know I was playing by ear). But when I ran out of tunes that I could remember, I resorted to playing whatever I was feeling on the inside (I later discov-ered the more technical term: improvisation). The music flowed straight from my heart. It was unlike any feeling I had ever felt before. Words can't begin to describe it, but it was as if the music presented me with an ability to tap into the deepest parts of my soul. To soothe, comfort, and heal—no adrenaline rush from any street activity could even have come close.

I was h-o-o-k-e-d. Night after night, the piano assumed the role of becoming my escape from reality, and anywhere I heard music, I followed. One afternoon as I wandered past the house of Eddie Lewis, the local barber in Sinclair Heights, I saw him walk out onto his front steps with a trumpet in hand. I stood there mesmerized as he blasted a tune. After he headed back inside, I couldn't help but run after him to ask how he did it. It was unbelievable to learn that you could create all of those notes using only three valves. Right then and there, I decided I wanted to play trumpet. Getting one was pretty much out of the question though, because I knew Daddy couldn't afford it. I did some digging and found out that my junior high school had some instruments available to borrow before and after class. Unfortunately, they didn't have a trumpet, so I started messing around with the violin and clarinet for a bit. After learning the basics, I jumped into percussion, sousaphone, B flat baritone horn, E flat alto peck horn, French horn, tuba, and trombone. If it made music, I wanted to play it.

One afternoon, a kid named Junior Griffin, who played the C melody sax, showed up at the common area of the rec hall with his horn and we started jamming together. He was on sax and I was on piano. A local music teacher, Joseph Powe, who led a Navy swing band that occasionally played at the rec center, took note of my interest in music and invited me to join an a cappella singing group, the Challengers. Mr. Powe also happened to be the former director of a famous Black gospel choir, Wings Over Jordan, so I dove right in. Our group started singing for tips on the streets of Bremerton, and even put on a little concert at the Cecil B. Moore Theater, which was my very first gig. We sang gospel songs like "Dry Bones" and "The Old Ark's a-Moverin." I can tell you right now that I wasn't the best singer, but I wasn't about to let that stop me.

During rehearsals at Mr. Powe's home, I couldn't help but notice all the books he had lying around—from Glenn Miller on arranging to Frank Skinner on film scoring. I had never heard of those professions, but the books kept opening my eyes to a world of musical possibilities. I had a voracious appetite for understanding where music could take me, so when he asked if I could babysit his kids one day, I immediately said, "Yes," just so I could spend more time reading. Every babysitting gig I buried myself in the pages on his shelves and tried to figure out what a G clef was and why a B flat trumpet had to play a whole tone above the concert note. I may not have been a five-star babysitter, but discovering this new world of music provided me with insight beyond my existing reality.

After World War II, Black people weren't welcome in Sinclair Heights anymore, because it was basically built as a temporary housing project. Around the same time, Daddy's work at the Naval Shipyard carpentry shop also dried up. So, with the little money he had, he moved us all to a tiny house at 410 22nd Avenue in the Central District of Seattle. Waymond, Lloyd, and I stayed in the attic, while the other siblings, Daddy, and Elvera (the stepmother) were stuffed into two downstairs bedrooms.

Much to my surprise, Seattle turned out to be an absolute music mecca, and all I wanted to do was absorb every inch of it. If it got me out of the house, you better believe I was there. Up and down Jackson Street, from 1st to 14th, and along Madison Street, between 21st and 23rd, I had every possible style of music at my fingertips. I'm talking about bebop, blues, R&B, pop music, you name it. And to top it off, after I graduated from Robert E. Coontz Junior High in downtown Bremerton, I made my way over to the progressive James A. Garfield High School across the street from my house. That's where everything clicked. Parker Cook, the school's music teacher, sensed my outsized interest in the trumpet and allowed me to have free and full rein in the band room. It seemed as though I had waited a lifetime to finally put my hands on this one instrument, so I didn't mind the fact that it was a bit worn. To me, it was like striking gold. I picked it up, positioned it the way I remembered barber Eddie Lewis had, blew out a sound, and sat completely still in the aftermath of the blare. It was a rather dull noise, soft with no vibrato, as I hadn't yet learned the necessary technique. But despite my lack of skill, I had a subconscious attraction to the sound which piqued my curiosity. And, most important, Mr. Cook continuously provided me with the space to envision what I could be—more than a baby gangster from the projects.

One cold night, as I tossed and turned on my cot in the attic, I peered out of what my brothers and I called our "dream window." With only blackberry bushes and piles of trash for a view, you had to have a big imagination up there. The cold was debilitating, and as I looked out, trying to will the chill away, all I could see were rats running out from under the house into the yard, making the escape that I so badly wanted to make. In one swift move I grabbed something to write on and sketched out some makeshift staff paper. With a basic knowledge of music composition from my readings, I began to jot down a piece that was reflective of a dream I had about flying away to some far-off land. I poured everything I had learned from Mr. Powe's books and Mr. Cook's classroom onto my paper that night, and took it with me everywhere I went so that I could work out the kinks on any piano I found, from the band-room piano at Garfield High to the Washington Social and Educational Club after hours. Working on this piece, combined with the hope that my mentors provided me with, pushed me toward a hopeful feeling that my composition, "From the Four Winds," was my ticket out of there.

I never had any control over my living situations, my nightmares, the angry folks who still called me the N-word, and no control over my future (or so I thought). However, nobody could tell me what tempo to begin my composition in or how many substitute chord changes I could play around with. The deeper I delved into composition and trumpet playing, the more I began to see what was possible, both personally and musically. Retrospectively, "From the Four Winds" is on the lesser-known end of the spectrum when it comes to my body of work, but, to me, it is one of the most important because it gave me my first ounce of confidence as a composer.

It's important to recognize that the only reason I was able to envision a way out of the situation I was born into was because I was exposed to a hopeful path. Mine came in the form of creativity, but I want you to know that being creative isn't simply a matter of what type of brushstroke you use to establish form on a canvas, or what key changes you write into a song. Rather, I believe that survival is also an act of creativity. It's a matter of seeking out new ways to stay inspired, and creating paths that lead to a better future for yourself, and in turn, others.

The increasing amount of exposure to the idea that I could steer my life in a positive direction was enough for me to cling to and fight for. Subconsciously, that sense of hope slowly began to permeate other areas of my mind, body, and soul, and created space for an unexpected amount of potential. In fact, most of my grades in school were terrible before I started delving into music; it was as if the passion that I discovered unlocked a hidden ability in me to thrive, instead of just existing to get by. My thoughts were no longer consumed by purposeless activities, but by dedicated curiosity. It was as if someone had lit a flame within me and I could finally see what had been lurking in the shadows.

As I reflect on that period of my life, it would be negligent of me to simply say that I found music and in turn "escaped the hood." There were a great deal of moving parts: from Mrs. Ayres unlocking the rec center for me, to Mr. Powe's bookshelf, to the chance encounter with Eddie Lewis and his trumpet, to Mr. Cook's band room at Garfield High. The combination of all these elements served as a filter for the pollution of my surroundings, pushing me closer to the clarity I never knew I could experience. With that in mind, I can only imagine how many people are out there with undiscovered potential or talent because they've never experienced a tangible sense of hope.

Although I found that spinet piano as a result of breaking and entering, I'm grateful for the end result, because it absolutely saved my life. Looking back, I know that if I had spent my waking moments still striving for a sense of belonging in a gang, instead of the band room, I'm confident that I would have been taken out a long time ago. Youth is an extremely impressionable time of life, and while that can be a great asset, it can also be detrimental to your development if the things you are molding into don't serve your best interest. Hear me when I say that this doesn't only apply to my economically disadvantaged brothers and sisters; it applies to each and every human being. You could have it all, in a material sense, but if you're assimilating to the wrong crowd or not allowing the right things to come in, then you only block yourself from your potential. And to those of you who have taken a few more trips around the sun, as I have, age is not an exemption for this rule. While you may be more settled in your path, I believe that the statute of limitations for all personal traumas holding you back has expired (or should expire). If your current position isn't what you envisioned, I'd encourage you to assess your past to understand how that plays into who you've become today.

Life is a beautiful responsibility, but it's also a beautiful burden. It's ultimately yours to protect for the time you've been given. Whether you're on the side of seeking out hope or in a position to help spread it, I'm telling you right now: You are more courageous than you think, wiser than you know, and more loved than you could ever imagine.

As complicated as it has been, I'm grateful for my path and for the combination of events that have taken place to help me uncover the dirt that I was buried under from the start. I thank God for that piano. I thank God for Mr. Powe, for Mrs. Ayres, and for Mr. Cook, some of the earliest influences on what would eventually become my future. The flame within still burns to this day, and it is the reason I am often able to see through polluted environments.

Hope may be presented in different forms, but it's always in the fine print. It's not about starting out on top, but it's about realizing how far you have to climb and then never giving up. And when I say never, I mean it. I don't believe you ever reach the top, and well, if you do, you might not be dreaming big enough.

If you can see it you can be it.

YOU

GOTTA

GO

TO KNOW

As we just discussed, being exposed to more than what is available to you in your immediate sphere of life is an important variable in the equation of growth. To put it simply, you gotta "go to know." You've got to step outside of what is familiar to you because falling prey to comfort only prevents you from experiencing the fullness of life that different people, places, and languages have to offer. Not only will you be able to see more of the beauty that this planet has to offer, but, as a creator, you will in turn be able to reflect that in your art.

Immersing yourself in the native culture of a particular place is an incredibly important aspect of life as it ultimately prevents you from trying to force your culture onto everybody else. We are all guilty of trying to compress others into what we are familiar with, but it's time to get rid of the I-me-mine mentality, and start focusing on "we," "us," and "ours." Not only does it make our communal human experience a more meaningful one, but it also provides a richer well of knowledge to draw from, making us more creative individuals.

For example, my creativity comes from my experiences, and without experiencing more of the world, I would only be able to create from a limited perspective. Think about "We Are the World," the 1985 charity single we produced that went on to become the bestselling single of all time. There's no way I could've been a part of that if I didn't truly immerse myself in what the world was going through, including poverty, hunger, strife, and a myriad of ailments. How can you expect to create art that transcends cultural boundaries if you yourself aren't even able to relate to someone on the other side of your city? One of the main ways I have been able to achieve this is by traveling and directly immersing myself in other cultures—from the language to the food to the music.

There are so many flavors in this rainbow we call life, and I hope you get to taste every single one of them. I'm grateful to have learned the lesson behind "go to know" at a very young age, and the best part is that you do not have to be a student for this lesson to apply. In fact, I've learned more on the road than I ever could've imagined. I've never stopped opening my heart and mind, and I think anyone who puts an expiration date on exploration because of their age puts themselves at an extreme disadvantage. When we close ourselves off to knowledge, we close ourselves off to our potential and true human connection. Come back with me to the early 1950s and I'll show you what I mean.

Colored. White.

Two simple words that possessed the unfortunate power to dictate your every move, from which entrance to which bathroom you could use. They told you exactly where you *weren't* welcome. I knew that was simply how it was growing up in the thirties, forties, fifties, and sixties, but man, it smacked me hard in the face when I went on my very first American tour in 1951. My composition "From the Four Winds" caught the attention of my idol, the great bandleader Lionel Hampton, and I was invited to join his big band.

We hit the road hard, doing three hundred one-nighters that year, traveling all across America, from Tulsa to Wichita to Albuquerque—you name it. With a bus full of Black musicians in the fifties, we always had to have a white bus driver because we couldn't have stopped at restaurants otherwise; the driver would have to go and either make sure the coast was clear for us to go in, or bring the food out for the band.

I'll never forget crossing the border into Texas around three A.M., hungry as hell, having to stop at six different places trying to find something to eat, only for the driver to tell us it was simply too dangerous to get off the bus. We couldn't do anything about it, so we continued to drive with our stomachs on empty, and finally made it to Dallas three hours later. Upon entering the city, we passed by one of the local churches, and right there on the steeple was a long rope tied to the top with an effigy of a Black man hanging from it—basically a signal to passersby that "If you're Black, don't stop. Don't even think about coming here." We kept moving.

Finding a place to stay was a whole other story; it was an all-around inconvenient and painful process anywhere we traveled in America. After we played a gig at a club that profited off of our name on the marquees, we'd have to exit through the "colored" door and go find a "colored" motel with vacancies. One night we were traveling through Newport News, Virginia, when there were absolutely no openings at the "colored" motels, so my roommate Little Jimmy Scott and I had to sleep in a funeral parlor with dead bodies all around us.

The only way to find some relief for a week at a time was to go and play the Chitlin' Circuit (the name given to the Black-owned theaters, jook joints, dance halls, nightclubs, and venues that were safe for Black entertainers to perform at during segregation). We'd hit them all up, including the Apollo in New York, the Uptown in Philadelphia, the Regal in Chicago, the Royal in Baltimore, and the Howard Theatre in Washington, D.C. These were the only places Black acts could settle down, so we wound up playing those venues about four times each that year.

On one hand, we were celebrated entertainers, but as soon as we stepped offstage and put our trumpets and saxophones down, we were once again reduced to the color of our skin. My daddy always used to remind me of the phrase "Not one drop of my self-worth depends on your acceptance of me." So, my old buddy Ray Charles (who I met back in Seattle when I was fourteen and he was sixteen) and I used to repeat that to each other when we were dealing with racism; it was the only mindset that got us through. However, even with the strength and power that those words held, they didn't make us bulletproof. No matter how I looked at it, what we endured on a daily basis was deeply hurtful. It really struck me even more to see these older jazz cats, whom I looked up to, stripped of their humanity time and time again.

In total, I did three years with Hamp (Lionel's nickname). When I first joined though, some of these cats had been on the road for thirty-plus years dealing with the same type of treatment. It may have gone against our natural instincts to walk through that every single day, when we could've just stayed home with people who looked the same as us, but we still chose to travel and perform because it was our form of freedom. Yes, it sure slapped our dignity right in the face, but at our core, we knew that our music was so much more powerful than any restriction that was placed on where we could or couldn't go. Most important, we stayed unified, and when you operate as a unit, you learn to develop a collective set of coping mechanisms in order to prevent the anger from bubbling over. Humor and wit, coupled with our passion for music, was truly how we powered through. There was this running joke on the road that whenever we were confronted with the statement "We don't serve 'N-words' here," we'd simply laugh and say, "Cool, we don't eat 'em." We couldn't let them take us out like that, so we had to take our mindset into our own hands.

In contrast with the division of the country, one of the most beautiful parts of that '51 tour, and the jazz community in general, was the camaraderie with the other musicians. Since I was the youngest one at eighteen years old, some of the older cats would always be pullin' me aside to drop some advice. The phrase that they'd all say—everyone from Count Basie, to Coleman Hawkins, to Benny Carter—was, "Youngblood, step into my office for a few ticks. Let me pull your coat" (slang for "Come over here. Let me teach you something."). That's when I learned why God gave us two ears and one mouth: because we're supposed to listen twice as much as we talk. Conversely, if he wanted us to talk more than we listen, he would've given us two mouths! At that age, I had to learn real quick that when someone knows what they're talking about, it's time to shut up. That lesson proved to be important because if you didn't catch on to the rules of the road, you'd be left out to dry.

One of the most important pieces of advice I received was from the legendary saxophonist Ben Webster (nicknamed "the Brute") when I was twenty. Right before I toured to Europe for the first time with Hamp in 1953, Ben pulled me aside and said, "Youngblood. Wherever you go in the world with Hamp, I want you to learn thirty to forty words in every language of every country you go to. If you learn the language, that'll take you to the food and the music. Then I want you to listen to the same music they listen to and eat the same food they eat because the soul of a country is identified by its music, food, and language. You've simply got to go to know." I kept his advice in my back pocket and anxiously waited to put it into practice on the road.

After our band arrived at the Palais d'Orsay station in Paris around eight P.M., via train from Switzerland, we were greeted with a breathtaking view of a crimson sky hugging the silhouette of the Eiffel Tower. It was one of the most beautiful sights I had ever seen in my twenty years of life. The city didn't disappoint either. Paris was a jazz musician's *dream*. As a result of Black soldiers bringing jazz to Europe after World War I, the French welcomed us with open arms, which was completely different from how we were treated back home in the United States. It was the most glorious time. Not only was I playing as a member in one of my idol's bands in a place that accepted us for who we were, but being on the road was like getting to attend a traveling music university.

At the very first restaurant the band stopped at in France, I was determined to follow Ben's instructions to learn the language, so I attempted to read the menu. When I looked down at all of the foreign words on the page, the only thing I could make out was "beefstek and potages." I thought to myself, "Well, you can never go wrong with some beefsteak and potatoes!" The dish turned out to be a type of porridge soup. I continued to make mistakes all over that city, but learning how to speak a local language, though, was an indescribably fulfilling experience. I started off small, and, even though it felt intimidating at first, things started to make sense little by little. A word here, a word there—it all added up. From France to Sweden to Greece to Pakistan, I was determined to communicate as the locals did.

Slowly but surely, over the course of my travels with the band, this process opened my eyes to how humans communicate across borders. Ben was right: Learning a bit of the language took me straight to the food. Once I could finally read what was on the menu, I could accurately express what I wanted to order. From paella to shepherd's pie and feijoada, to chicken marbella and sole meunière, my mind was blown as it processed the unparalleled tastes as well as the art behind each chef's creation. The fact that these cooks knew which spices to blend so that there was a harmony and delicate balance to each dish opened my eyes to the creativity that was involved in cooking—definitely a level up from the survival food I was used to eating back home.

Learning about the variety of foods in the world and the usage of staple ingredients that were common to a specific culture brought me to the understanding that food and music are inextricably linked.

Think about it. What's the loudest and most prominent instrument in the orchestra?

The piccolo!

Now, think about cooking. What's the strongest flavor that ascends above any other?

Lemon!

I believe the piccolo's culinary equivalent is lemon. It doesn't matter how much hot sauce and garlic or anything else you include in a dish, lemon will take them all out, just like the piccolo can in a symphony orchestra. Flavors of food and fundamentals of music are very closely related, and it taught me to cook like an orchestrator and orchestrate like a chef. The deeper I got, and the more I understood how to mix different flavors and sounds, the more combinations I was able to play around with.

In a way, I felt as though Ben handed me the secret code to life. It absolutely flipped me upside down. Having originally come from the ghetto in Chicago, I only knew what was familiar to me. After experimenting abroad with new languages, food, and music, though, an entirely new world opened up, breathing more life into my own. I didn't have to learn a whole language, or eat all of the food, or hear all of the music. I just had to be open to it in order to understand and appreciate what made different regions tick.

Traveling helped me see things differently. More than anything, it also helped me to *be seen* differently. When we toured France, the French accepted us for who we were—as musicians, and not just Black musicians. They took care of us, loved our music, and loved our people. We wouldn't have jazz if it weren't for the French. If anything, they fought for jazz at Congo Square during the time of slavery, and all throughout Europe afterward. It was the first time in my life that I felt free as a Black man and a musician. It wasn't about what you looked like; it was simply about "Can you play sucka?" They showed me what it meant to have a genuine love and respect for differences.

France evokes many of the warmest, most vivid memories of my entire life. In a way, Europe helped me define myself as a young musician and find my place in the world. It helped me get out of America where all of my problems were right in front of my face, due to the *color* of my face, and made it impossible to separate my struggles from my music. Seeing the joy as well as the suffering that various people were experiencing abroad showed me that I have more in common with my fellow brothers and sisters on the other side of the planet than I previously realized. Traveling became a celebration of cultural differences. It opened my soul and mind to a much larger world than the box that racism had tried to keep me in.

Having experienced that type of cross-cultural freedom for the very first time in Europe, I made it a goal to try and seek that out in my subsequent travels, and I haven't stopped since. As an added bonus to Ben's lesson, appreciating a city's culture through the language, food, and music of its inhabitants gave me a new perspective on the past, present, and future. Reading about the history of a specific group of people is completely different from *feeling* the history as you walk through monuments and war sites or sit with a local to hear their perspective on how the past has shaped the present.

As an American, it's upsetting to know that, at the time of this writing, the United States does not have a Ministry of Culture. It's reflective of a poisonous societal mindset that history and culture are irrelevant. Well, I'm telling you, culture is anything *but* irrelevant. You've got to know where you came from in order to get where you want to go. Without that foundation, you won't know who you are, and you sure can't expect to create truthfully without knowing the truth. Additionally, the handprints of cross culturalization can be found all over modern art if you just take a deeper look.

For example, most of the time when I ask artists where breakdancing came from, they say the Bronx. Wrong! It came from Capoeira, a type of martial arts disguised as dance, developed thousands of years ago by enslaved Africans from Angola and Brazil. A friend of mine who choreographed the Rio 2016 Olympic Games set out to demonstrate this concept by having breakdancers from the Bronx perform, followed by Brazilian dancers doing Capoeira. It's completely evident that every step the breakdancers performed was an evolution of this art form.

And then when I ask artists where rap came from, they usually can't give me a straight answer. Well, it came from the Imbongi, the Griots, and the Oral Historians of Africa. From our music to our slang, it came from those who paved the way for us. Lester Young was calling Count Basie "homeboy" ninety years ago! Doo wop, bebop, hip-hop, laptop—it's all part of the same evolution. People don't usually talk about why we ended up with bebop, doo-wop, and hip-hop, but that's because they're all a sociological result of a really painful existence. Our music wasn't born out of the East Coast; it was born out of slavery. That should radically change the way we view our art.

I believe music is the heartbeat of life because it has the ability to speak to all types of people, regardless of color or origin. In fact, records show that the first recorded piece of poetry in the style of rap was "Kinesiska Muren," a song that dates back to Europe in the early 1900s from Swedish author, artist, composer, and singer, Evert Taube. He and his son, Sven-Bertil Taube, were curators of folk songs from Stockholm, and "Kinesiska Muren" was later redone by Dag Vag and made Top 10 on the May 1981 Billboard Hits of the World Chart.

You can't allow yourself to get so comfortable to the point where you wear ignorance as a badge and think it's OK to not know what happened before you. It's never cool not to know. I tell the hip-hoppers that all the time. We can't afford to raise a generation of creators who think they're the only people on the planet or the first ones to inhabit it. People who don't know their history, or how to celebrate cultural differences, are simply left with stereotypes and preconceived ideas, which is a large part of why racism still exists today.

That's why I have such a hard time hearing rappers use the N-word in their music. I know you might think I sound a bit old-school but I only say it because I lived through it. If people had actually felt the depth of the pain accompanied by that word, they probably wouldn't use it so carelessly in their art. I've heard it used many different ways, and it's as though artists feel that if we keep playing with it, the word won't mean anything anymore. The original word, derived from Eritrean roots, once symbolized a type of monarch, and was meant to be a term of endearment. But now, no matter how you look at it, there's too much subjectivity out there to be that nonchalant with using the word in lyrics—lyrics that people of all backgrounds will be singing aloud.

Everything we do is an extension of the history that came before us, and if we don't recognize it, we're in danger of repeating some of the same nonsense that went down in the past. It's a beautiful thing to reflect and learn, rather than to reject and repeat.

For my eighty-fifth birthday, my team at Quincy Jones Productions and I went to Europe for an orchestral tour through London, Paris, Budapest, and Switzerland. It was incredible to see people from every age, race, religion, and class fill up each venue, night after night. I've been traveling in the name of music for more than seventy years now, and witnessed over and over again how music has the ability to unite people from all walks of life. That reality speaks louder than any words I could write on a page. Regardless of where I am in the world, usually when I finish a recording session with collaborators, we go to each other's houses to cook for each other, play new music, and talk and laugh together. It always creates an atmosphere for genuine connection, and further space for creativity and musical experimentation to take place.

To this day, I've continued to take Ben Webster's advice seriously throughout all of my stops and have learned the basics of close to twenty-seven languages: French, Swedish, Serbo Croatian, Farsi, Iranian, Turkish, Greek, Russian, Katakana, and so many more. It's truly the most beautiful gift to feel at home anywhere I go in the world and to see people for who they really are. Whether it's the difference in a word's meaning based upon the placement of an accent, the differences in flavors of ingredients, or the differences in world music, you've got to open your heart and your mind to be able to understand and celebrate them all.

So, if you only take away one thing from this Note, please hear me when I say, you gotta "go to know." *Je t'aime dix mille fois!*

ESTABLISH

YOUR

GUIDEPOSTS

NOTE

C

Now that you're all packed for your next adventure, I want to share another lesson with you that I discovered to be of the utmost importance during one of my travels: Establish guideposts in order to stay grounded in who you are. If you haven't properly set up a foundation for yourself, there's really no point in trying to learn how to become the best musician, or businesswoman, or actor, or whatever it is you want to be because it'll come crashing down once you reach the first intersection of struggle and desperation. If you don't know who you are from the start, you'll lose yourself, at best, and let someone else decide for you, at worst.

I see way too many cats out there getting caught up in the excitement of fame, only to be met with all-consuming depression on the other side, often because they've lost sight of who they are and why they even started creating in the first place. Talent comes with responsibility, and managing your gifts can become a burden if you have yet to identify how you will respond to external pressures. With technology and social media making it easier than ever to grow your own following, our society has placed an incredibly alarming amount of emphasis on surface-level matter, often neglecting the individual person as a whole. Now that such platforms are here to stay, there's an added layer of scrutiny to every situation. Not only are the embarrassing moments or failures of life dealt with on a personal level, but they are also publicly magnified. That's enough to destroy anyone without a foundation.

This is why it's necessary to set up guideposts that routinely remind you of who you are, apart from the distractions of life. Although I have yet to find a one-size-fits-all method, I've personally found the practice of affirmations to be quite effective. I'm not going to get all spiritual on you, but there's something to be said for the power of repetition. If you don't want outside forces defining who you are, then you've got to combat those forces just as often with words and actions that remind you of your identity. Your success in any field is only as strong as the foundation that you create for yourself.

I wish I'd known this when I was twenty-six, the time I led a band of eighteen musicians, and a total travel party of thirty-three people, on a bootstrapped tour through Europe, with nothing to offer but my broken promises and a full-blown identity crisis. I came alarmingly close to taking my own life, because for a moment there, I lost sight of who I was. In order to understand how I got to this point though, and, more important, how I got out of it, I've got to take you back to where it began.

Free and Easy. 1959.

By this time, I was married to and had a baby (Jolie) with my high school sweetheart, Jeri Caldwell. We moved to New York after I returned to the United States from touring Europe with Lionel Hampton's big band. I had been in and out of various bands and was eager to start my own. On top of that, there was a growing demand for big bands. Because of the way airline travel was developing, it was predicted that by 1964, bands could be doing one-nighters in England or Germany with the same regularity as New York and Pittsburgh. Europe promised to become an important part of any band's itinerary, so it seemed like the perfect time to realize my dream of forming a big band.

I was determined to hire the best possible musicians. However, trying to find players who would be willing to go on the road for a whole month with no guaranteed gigs was a great way to land myself a grand 'ol "No." After weeks of keeping my ears open for opportunities, I got in touch with the renowned talent scout and record executive at Columbia Records, John Hammond. I knew he would understand what I was trying to do. I told him about my idea and he referred me to Stanley Chase, who was in need of a music director. Stanley was the producer of *Free and Easy*, a Harold Arlen/Johnny Mercer show that was slated to open in Europe with Harold Nicholas. I contacted Stanley, and after discussing my plan and his simultaneous search for a music director, we worked out a deal in which I'd fill the role and assemble my dream band to hit the road as part of the musical.

The plan was to take the show over to Europe for a few months to rehearse in Paris. Then we would tour to London, where Sammy Davis Jr. would take over for Harold Nicholas. After we perfected every scene, we'd come back to New York and hit Broadway. Being the music director for a Broadway show had been a dream of mine ever since I started learning about the profession as a kid, and I wasn't about to let this once-in-a-lifetime opportunity slip through my fingers.

With a guaranteed gig for my band in the bag, I picked up the phone and asked every musician I had ever dreamed of playing with to join me. Not only did I have a show lined up, but I also promised them I'd book us extra side gigs while we were out there. After a few days, I rounded up an absolute killer big band and was set on making it the best group on the planet.

In October 1959, *DownBeat* published an article about *Free and Easy* stating, "The show is dripping with firsts. Since Quincy Jones is writing the score for the show, it will be the first Broadway musical ever scored by a jazz composer and arranger, possibly the first that ever used a jazz orchestra [onstage] in place of a pit band. It will also be the first Broadway show that ever went through its tryout performances in

Europe instead of the customary Boston, Hartford, Bridgeport, and Philadelphia."

The *New York Times* wrote, "Mr. Jones says with the fervor of a novitiate, 'We're either going to rock the boat or sink it.'" And boy was I determined to rock the boat.

Once we made it overseas, we were unstoppable. For two months, we rehearsed the show front to back. After tightening up every loose screw, it was time to debut on the road. With our full cast and crew of nearly seventy people, we traveled from Brussels to Holland, and then to Paris for our opening at the Alhambra theater.

But, unfortunately, our show coincided with the height of the Algerian War of Independence. The sound of machine gun fire rang throughout the city of Paris. Police and soldiers roamed the streets without pause, and there was a notice on the front page of the *Herald Tribune* that said, "Any swarthy-complexioned person is advised to stay off the street after six o'clock in the evening." And man, we had more than swarthy complexions. Although France had been viewed as a refuge from American racism, especially for us jazz musicians, that didn't mean we darker-skinned folks were exempt from getting caught in the middle of the war between Caucasian French and Algerian French citizens.

Whether we were going to the theater or heading home, many of us were stopped by the police. I'll never forget when this happened to me one night, after I caught a ride to a friend's (the great pianist Art Simmons) home. When I stepped out of the car, I was greeted by the sound of a gun clicking right by my head;

once I saw it was the police pointing their pistol in my direction, my immediate reaction was to put my hands up. Such an environment filled with fear began to permeate every corner of the city, and people were afraid to leave their homes and go to the store, let alone go to the theater.

Before we even had a fair chance to prove the quality of our production, the show started losing money.

After assessing the financial damage, the producer told the cast that we only needed to make it through two more months in Paris. That arrangement would allow us to follow our original plan and go to London, then subsequently back to Broadway with Sammy Davis Jr. We fought tooth and nail to hang on to our slot at the Alhambra theater for about six weeks. With only fourteen days left to go, the producer gathered the cast and crew on a Thursday and broke the news: "The plane is leaving on Saturday. If any of you miss that flight, you're going to be stuck here."

I couldn't believe what I was hearing. I had assembled my dream big band and brought all of the musicians out to Paris to be a part of what was supposed to be one of the most remarkable road shows to date. On top of that, the band had found its sweet spot over the last four months of performing together. Notable critics had rated my band as number three on the list of top big bands, right after Duke Ellington and Count Basie. These jazz kings had ruled the game for a long time, so seeing my name next to these idols was a dream come true. We had also managed to release my self-conducted big band record, *Birth of a Band*, through Mercury Records. We were just starting to pull in rave reviews, and I knew that if we got back on that plane, all we would have after these months in Europe was a failed show and a record that wasn't properly toured.

As soon as I heard the producer's final decision, I gathered my band. I begged them to give me one day to figure out how to keep us together in Europe. I had already lined up two shows for us that weekend—one at L'Olympia in Paris and another in Stockholm—and I needed to find a way for us to finish those dates.

Within twenty-four hours, I had concocted a plan for how to keep the band working together in Europe. However, as soon as my words escaped my mouth and made their way into the hearts of my band members, I knew I had signed up for more than I bargained for.

Saturday came and went, and so did the cast and crew. Except my band and me. There were thirty-three people in total, including my eighteen musicians, some of their wives and kids, my own wife and baby, a classical opera singer from the show named Eli Hodges (who I had also hired to act as our assistant), a mother-in-law of one of the musicians, and two band members' dogs. Although we big band musicians were never in it for the money or fame, I still had to figure out how to pay them and cover their basic needs. So, after getting the band situated as best as I could for the next night, I hopped on the phone and went to work.

I made contact with a French promoter, who secured sixteen dates for us in France and promised cash advances on each of them. Knowing I had that money waiting for us, I chartered a raggedy li'l plane to take us to Stockholm, Sweden, to finish our gig over the weekend. However, when we returned to Paris, the French promoter had skipped town with our advances for the sixteen dates—he and our money were long gone. One thing that remained was the Algerian War. It was an incredibly unsafe climate to travel in, and I had no manager or booking agent. I had practically no experience booking a tour, if you could call it that since we were just gigging anywhere and everywhere I could find. I dragged us through Holland, Belgium, Italy, Yugoslavia, Finland, Austria, Germany, Sweden, back to Germany, then to France, Switzerland, and over to Portugal. We wandered around like vagabonds, traveling by bus, train, car, or foot.

While piecing together loose change to keep us fueled, I put in calls to friends far and wide to see if they needed a band. To my surprise, the concert promoter, Norman Granz, offered us a three-week slot opening for Nat King Cole's first European tour. Nat truly was one of the best musicians to have ever walked the earth, and getting to spend those three weeks on the road with him reassured me that I was doing the right thing. It also allowed me to earn some quick cash to keep us going. After we finished the dates with him though, I paid the musicians and found myself right where I was from the start. Broke. To be real, we were always broke, but now we were broke, broke.

The band looked like a bunch of street rats sitting on platforms of local train stations, while I stood off to the side calling in favors on the nearest pay phone. After we couldn't stay at the train station any longer, we slept on buses until I could secure our next gig. Although many of the band members were older than me by strides, I still had to provide. I had promised them that I would. The stress was piling on and I was in a constant state of panic, always waiting for loans to be wired so that I could at least get some of the families a hotel room.

Right when I thought we were truly done for, Brice Somers, chief executive of the Swiss office of Mercury Records International, along with his wife, Clare-Lise, paid for an entire train car to bail us out of Yugoslavia. After paying the band their salary, I had about $62,000 left over in Yugoslavian money, which was basically worthless outside of the country. I took a gamble and spent the entire sum on some train tickets to whatever cities I could think of. I was hoping that if we were at least already in a city that had open slots, we could secure gigs the night of. My hope was to recoup the Yugoslavian money, but it ain't no joke paying to transport a big band and their families, especially when you're not even sure you're going to land a paid gig at the final destination. If I guessed right about where we should go next, we had work. If I messed up, we'd sleep on the nearest bus or train, or I'd put them up in a motel until I could get something more permanent.

After about ten months of dragging thirty-three people across Europe and having to come up with $4,800 a week just to cover their basic needs, everything within me was shutting down. My mind, body, *and* soul. I had been alive for twenty-six years, but it felt as though the weight of the world had aged me threefold. Each of the musicians was starting to crack as well.

When we finally arrived at a local hotel for one night in Turku, Finland, I was at the end of my rope. I had begged and borrowed from everyone I could possibly think of and over-used every favor in the book. A big band completely stranded in Europe wasn't exactly the type of investment that people wanted to place their faith and/or money in. I had no way of getting the band home and had exhausted all of my sources of help.

Inside my room, I kept replaying the events of the last few months over and over in my mind. I couldn't accept the fact that my grand plan to tour my first big band didn't turn out as I had envisioned. I was angry. When I accepted the gig as the *Free and Easy* music director, I knew it would be life-changing, but not career-ending.

I wanted to escape. I needed to escape. The thought of having to pay back all of the money I had borrowed continued to cycle in my head and I calculated that I was worth more dead than alive.

To make matters worse, I had also received a letter from my father earlier that week pleading for me to write him back, since he hadn't heard from me in almost a full year. The realization that I had left behind my father and little brother, Lloyd, struck me to my core. I could hear the disappointment through the pages of his letter that had traveled thousands of miles to reach me. His birthday had recently passed, but there I was, stuck in Turku, Finland, without money to even send my father a simple reply. All I wanted to do was get up, go out, and mail him a birth-day card, but I knew that as soon as I walked out of there, I'd have to face what awaited me on the other side of the door.

The pressure of trying to financially support thirty-three people in a foreign country plus the pressure of being known as a failure was unbearable; it was the first time in my life that I contemplated suicide. Not only did I think about it, but I thought deeply about how I would do it. Anything seemed more enticing than the mounting pressure I was under every day.

With no alternatives, and as a last resort, I began to pray. I can't even tell you how long I sat idle on the precipice of life and death. Whether it was minutes or hours later, something that my father used to tell me when I was a child began to seep down into the lower echelons of my mind: "You were created for a purpose." I didn't know exactly what that purpose was, but as I remained, deep in a state of turmoil and prayer, it was as if a light switch flipped on—a switch that illuminated a new-found hope in an unknown future. Even if it was the last thing I did, I had to make one last attempt to keep going. Mentally and physically.

With barely enough strength to scroll through my mind's Rolodex of contacts, I decided to put in a call to one person I hadn't reached out to yet—Irving Green. Irving founded Mercury Records, the label I had released *Birth of a Band* through. I told him about my situation and that I had reached my end. He immediately sent me a $1,700 loan. If *he* was willing to help me out, I knew I really needed to figure something out.

Irving's loan gave me the confidence to get the band back to the United States, but logistically, I still needed a lot more money. I strategically planned my next moves, then asked my wife Jeri to help me reach out to Charlie Hansen, the co-owner of Silhouette Music (a music publishing company we had started together about five years earlier in 1954) to try and get an advance of $14,000 against my share of all my songs. Little did we know, fine print is called fine print for a reason and that $14,000 advance against my publishing was actually a 100-percent sale that would later cost me $105,000 to buy back.

Regardless, the sale provided me with just enough to get us all home on the USS *United States*, a slow boat from Le Havre, France. I had never cried in front of my band before, but man, there's a first time for everything. It was the most embarrassing feeling to look my bandmates in the eyes and know that I had completely let them down. On one hand, I was relieved to be back home, but on the other hand, I still felt the weight of disappointment. Although I tried to keep the band together once we returned to New York, the financial fallout of that tour still followed us. Some of those cats lost homes, others lost relationships, and some lost both. It was an immense burden to carry, and I knew that if I wasn't careful, I'd mentally find myself right back where I was, in that hotel room in Turku, Finland.

The whole ordeal proved to me how deceptively easy it is to fall into a trap of losing sight of myself. Above all, it awoke a sense of urgency in me to figure out how I would move forward. Under the veil of guilt, shame, and suicidal thoughts, I made a promise to recite affirmations to myself every single day. I didn't really know where to start because articulating my purpose in life seemed too daunting of a task, but I simply started with verbalizing and affirming the type of person I desired to be, in tandem with language about the standard of character I had already demonstrated. Over time, it gave way to a deeper sense of belief in my future, which extended far beyond myself. The beautiful thing about this practice is that the repetitiveness of it served to rewire my subconscious mind by mitigating negative thoughts that attempted to take control.

Although the language of my affirmations has changed as I too have grown, the heart and soul of my words remain the same. Today, they go a little something like this:

> *Our Father who art in Heaven, hallowed be thy name.*
> *Thy kingdom come thy will be done, on Earth as it is in*
> *Heaven. Give us this day our daily bread and forgive us*
> *our trespasses as we forgive those who trespass against*
> *us. Lead us not into temptation but deliver us from evil,*
> *for thine is the kingdom, and the power, and the glory,*
> *forever and ever. Amen. I have conscious divine intel-*
> *ligence and I have direct knowledge of truth. I know*
> *because God is guiding me. God is guiding me with a*
> *divine will to help me to continue to build a character*
> *that I can love, that I can respect, that I can believe in,*
> *and that I can live with eternally, so that I may always*
> *be there long and strong for my precious children and*
> *their precious children for whatever reason, and my*
> *precious friends and their precious children—and my*
> *beloved children all over the world. I've been at their*
> *side since the beginning, because I'm really one of them,*
> *and I know what it feels like to be a street rat. I thank*
> *God for letting me be there for these kids, and for having*

had mentors who believe in me. Having lost my mother at seven, I recognize that I came up like these kids, and I will always be one of them. So, allow me to guard and protect and improve my health, because without my health, nothing else matters. I will develop my worth to the world, and my God-given talents until I leave this planet. I promise you I will.

I can't even begin to imagine what would've happened if I gave up on myself that day in my hotel room. I'm not sure what kind of legacy I would have left, but it would probably have played to the tune of a twenty-six-year-old kid who got a big band stranded in Europe. Believe me, it's easier said than done, but life is worth living. I've lived it and I ain't planning on stopping any time soon. If you're waiting until after your back is against the wall to establish your guideposts, the odds are sure to be in favor of your opponent. So, figure out what your guideposts look like for you, and set them up *early*. And when I say early, I'm not referring to age; it doesn't matter how long you've been on this planet because, sure, the past is the past, but the future is also the future. There's always time to get on the right track.

I'd be lying through my teeth if I said it has been free and easy after *Free and Easy* because it wasn't, and it still isn't—but please never give up. Although it took me a full seven years to pay off the amount of debt I owed from that tour, now that I look back, the years following have undoubtedly been much brighter than that period in my life. In fact, after I returned to New York, I got a real job for the first time in my life; I was an A&R (artists and repertoire) for Mercury Records, hired by Irving Green to help pay back my debt. Later on at that company, I became the first Black executive, as vice president, at a major record label. I also found Lesley Gore, whom I wound up producing eighteen hits with, including "It's My Party" and "You Don't Own Me." Funny enough, one of the songs I bought back from my Silhouette Music catalogue was "Soul Bossa Nova," which I subsequently released in 1960. A mere thirty-seven years later it would become the theme song to the *Austin Powers* franchise, beginning in 1997 with *International Man of Mystery*.

Speaking of mysteries, there's no telling what life might throw your way. But what should remain firm is your foundation. I'm not here to tell you what to do. I just want to tell you what has worked for me with the hope that it will inspire you to keep on keepin' on, and never give up—on your art, your dreams, your life. With a general understanding that our thoughts play an important role in the direction of our paths, it's essential to remain proactive in training those thoughts to continue pointing north, with the assistance of guideposts, whatever form they may come in for you. Personally, not a single day passes that I don't start my waking moments with my affirmations—the ultimate navigation system that has helped me not only *make* it to more than eighty-eight, but also *live* to more than eighty-eight. I pray you will, too.

ALWAYS BE PREPARED FOR A GREAT OPPORTUNITY

NOTE

C#

As the saying goes, "The only time you'll see 'success' before 'work' is in the dictionary." And you can say that again. The underlying principle of this statement reminds me of Thomas Edison's quote: "Success is ten percent inspiration and ninety percent perspiration." He really hit the nail on the head, because achieving success in any field, both professionally and personally, takes hard work. You can't sit around expecting opportunities to come your way; and when you ultimately receive them, you've got to be prepared to deliver. In fact, the dictionary definition of an opportunity is "a situation or condition favorable for attainment of a goal." Keep in mind—nowhere in that definition does it guarantee success. It only asserts that opportunities provide beneficial situations or conditions for action. So, what comes next? Hard work.

For as long as I can remember, my daddy would tell me every day, "Once a task has just begun, never leave it 'til it's done. Be the labor great or small, do it well or not at all." It didn't matter what the task was, I just knew that I needed to complete it to the best of my abilities. It became ingrained in my work ethic and has served me well over the years. Throughout my career, I have become the go-to for producing, composing, arranging, and just about anything that I've applied myself to because of my diligence. A great work ethic is an asset that will undoubtedly carry you through every phase of life because it is ultimately what sets you apart from the rest of your peers who are satisfied with getting a job done, but not very well.

In fact, my biggest fear has always been *not* being prepared for a great opportunity. "Fear" is a bad word in my book, because it's helpless. When you allow yourself to settle into a mindset of fear, you default to the assumption that you're not capable, or worthy enough to handle the task at hand. That's a risky place to be in, because instead of allowing yourself to prove that you *are* capable, you convince yourself that you aren't, before you even get started. But if you're prepared for anything that might get thrown your way, then nothing can scare you.

But don't get it twisted now. Fearlessness doesn't mean perfection. I'll be the first to tell you that I've made more mistakes than I can count. I failed hard and fast, but I found value in my mistakes, because they taught me what to watch out for the next time around. Just don't make the same mistake twice because that could determine whether or not you get asked to come back a second time, or get passed up for somebody else.

As my daddy repeatedly taught me, if you commit to something, you gotta go *all* the way with it. If you take a good look around, you'll find that a lot of people ideate but not many of them execute. It's a long road from ideation to execution. You have to be emotionally ready to put the required energy into whatever it is you are striving for because, if you don't, you'll hop into a vehicle with no gas. For many of us out there, we can't afford to miss that first shot. Always be prepared for a great opportunity.

Whenever I reflect on how I learned this lesson, I immediately go back to 1958 when I got the call of a lifetime to work with the great Frank Sinatra. But first, we've got to make a quick pit stop in high school so you get the full picture.

Back in 1948, when my band teacher, Parker Cook, let me have free rein over the band room at Garfield High in Seattle, I met a kid named Charlie Taylor who I quickly became friends with. We'd practice our instruments together day after day, and shortly thereafter, we decided to start a band. We aspired to be just like the big bands we'd heard on the radio, and recruited a whole mix of players to join us. We ran that group like it was our J-O-B and after a short while, we got our first gig playing the YMCA on 23rd and Madison. We were over the moon having made $7 apiece, but we didn't think playing music could be a real job—until we were approached by a local bandleader, named Bumps Blackwell, who asked if he could front the band. Bumps wasn't much older than us, but he had a great ear for talent and a *real* talent for promoting whatever it was that caught his ear in the first place.

Although Bumps fronted a few different groups and we were only his junior band, he made us into real showstoppers—just like our jazz idols we'd hear on the radio. From Charlie Parker to Dizzy Gillespie, we knew all the major names in bebop, which is why we completely lost our cool one day when Bumps delivered the news: "Billie Holiday (Lady Day) is coming to town and we're gonna back her up!" It was 1948, and we couldn't believe we were going to play for Lady Day, especially since Bumps had a senior band. As did most singers in those days, Billie traveled with a pianist who doubled as a music director who would hire local musicians in whatever city she was set to perform in. It was completely normal for her to need a backing band, but *completely* abnormal for a junior band to be chosen. When asked why he chose us, Bumps simply said, "It's because y'all can sight-read better than anybody else around here."

With only a few minutes to spare before showtime, fifteen-year-old me nervously stood there in the wings of the Eagles Auditorium, looking out at a packed house of nine hundred people, scared to the bone. After Billie's music director, the famous arranger and pianist Bobby Tucker, briefed our band on the quality of playing that he expected from us out there on stage, it was time. Billie sang like the true star we all expected her to be, but our band was so struck by her presence that we came out crankin' like a Mack truck long overdue for an oil change. Bobby leaned over at us from the piano, and professionally asserted beneath the volume of the music, "If you m-fers are gonna stand there gawking at Billie instead of reading the music, get off the bandstand and go buy a ticket." We may have started out wrinkled, but Bobby's words pressed us out real quick—we got it together in a matter of seconds. The concert turned out to be a huge success, and I was prepared to preserve the experience as a special memory and nothing else.

Little did I know, Bobby Tucker would return later that year—this time with the legendary Billy Eckstine—and ask for a repeat accompaniment from handpicked members of the Bumps Blackwell Junior Band, including myself. I was determined to prove my chops once again, minus that earlier mistake we first made when we backed Lady Day. After the show, I asked Bobby for feedback and told him how serious I was about my playing. I was once again prepared to store this once-in-a-lifetime experience as simply a memory and nothing else.

Fast forward to August 1957, when the performances I did with Bobby Tucker, Billie Holiday, and Billy Eckstine in '48 graduated from a memory to the catalyst for my next major career move. You see, Billy Eckstine was signed to the famous Barclay Records in Paris, owned by business genius Nicole Barclay and her husband Eddie Barclay. When Billy Eckstine heard that Nicole was looking for an American music director, he told her, "I know somebody. Call Quincy Jones. He's one of the best arrangers in New York." Bobby had kept in touch with me ever since that gig from when I was fifteen, but at twenty-four, still a kid in the jazz world, the call came as a complete surprise.

I wanted to set things up before sending back to New York for my baby, Jolie, and wife, Jeri, so with the offer in hand, I officially made the move to Paris to become the music director, arranger, and conductor for Barclay Records. Through this position, I was able to work with musicians I would've never had the opportunity to collaborate with in the United States otherwise, including the likes of Charles Aznavour, Stéphane Grappelli, Henri Salvador, Michel Legrand, Double Six, Andy Williams, and Sarah Vaughan. I also wound up writing arrangements for at least a few hundred dates for Eddie Barclay's fifty-five-piece resident orchestra. It was an experience of a lifetime that finally led me to *the* call.

One afternoon in 1958 when I was working with Eddie, we received a call from the office of Princess Grace of Monaco. They told Eddie, "Frank Sinatra is coming here to sing for the premiere of his movie, *Kings Go Forth*, and he wants you and Quincy to bring an orchestra to the Sporting Club in Monaco." I couldn't believe my ears. I mean, the man was pretty much the most famous artist on the planet! We ecstatically agreed, caught the train with Eddie's orchestra, and headed south to play behind Sinatra.

By that time, I had learned that it was important to approach each singer differently, in order to cater to their specific vocal range, instead of treating arranging as a one-size-fits-all approach. At twenty-five years old, I was determined to prove myself and learn exactly what it was that Frank wanted cooked up, in terms of arrangement and emotion. Frank's presence demanded attention as he strolled into rehearsal at the Monaco

Sporting Club with his "Swinging Lovers" hat cocked to the side. He asserted, "You've heard the records, you know what to do. You know where I'm coming from." We rehearsed the show with a full orchestra for four hours, and when we were done, Frank said, "Koo-koo," and walked out.

When the entire concert came to a close, he shook my hand and commented a mere, "Yeah, nice job, Q," (the first time anyone ever called me "Q") and was gone. This man was bottom-to-top buttoned up in business. I think I only exchanged a few sentences with Frank the whole night. I didn't even have a chance to thank him. I returned to Paris in a trance and was once again prepared to safeguard that performance as a permanent fixture in my memory and nothing more.

Fast forward to 1964.

I hadn't exchanged a single word with Frank since the night of our gig in Monaco. After almost six years of no contact, I thought he had long forgotten about me. But one afternoon, when I was working as the vice president of A&R at Mercury Records in New York (you know, the job I took to pay back my *Free and Easy* debt), I received a call from Hollywood. "Hey, Q, this is Francis. I'm in Hawaii directing a film called *None but the Brave*. I heard the record you did last year with Basie," he said, in reference to Bart Howard's "In Other Words (Fly Me to the Moon)," which I had arranged in 4/4 time (instead of 3/4) for some extra swing. "That's the way I'd like to do it too. Would you consider doing an album with Basie and me?"

With my heart just about ready to jump out of my chest, I said, "Man, is the pope a Catholic? You bet I will!"

"Koo-koo. My office will handle the details. See you in Kauai next week." *Click.*

After receiving further instructions from his team, I understood that Frank wanted me to arrange and conduct Count Basie's band, plus add a string section for his next album, *It Might as Well Be Swing*, which included "In Other Words (Fly Me to the Moon)."

I worked night and day to prove myself on that gig and delivered exactly what Frank wanted. He was so ecstatic with the outcome of the record that he took the music on the road, with me as his official conductor and arranger. Race wasn't an issue for him; Frank treated our band with profound respect and made sure to shine the spotlight on me and the rest of the musicians just as much as it shined on him. Frank and I became fast friends and the ultimate collaborative duo. He knew that if he needed an arrangement done, I would get it done exactly how he envisioned it. Whenever he'd have an issue with the orchestrations, I'd fix it immediately. In order to deliver, I made sure to learn the meaning behind his idiosyncrasies in order to achieve the type of groove that his songs deserved. If he was only lifting his foot about six inches to tap along to the beat, I could tell that we weren't swingin' hard enough. Whenever that happened, I told the drummer to pick up the back beat a little stronger until Frank lifted his foot up a whole foot and a half to stomp along to the beat.

I'm telling you, my work with Frank didn't happen by chance. It happened because I had sharpened my tools and mastered the craft I set out to pursue. I remember one time he told me, "That's just a little too dense up front in the first eight, of 'The Best Is Yet to Come,' Q." Within ten minutes, it was fixed. I had observed the pros for many years up until I began working with him, making sure to prepare myself to be the best conductor and arranger I could possibly be.

In 1966, I teamed up again with Frank for his first live album, *Sinatra at the Sands*, which we recorded in Las Vegas. Then in 1969, Buzz Aldrin and Neil Armstrong played our rendition of "Fly Me to the Moon" in outer space—making it the first song ever to be played on the moon—an experience I never could have dreamed up myself! I wound up working with Frank for nearly forty years, all the way up until his passing in 1998. Frank was more than a musical peer and friend. He was like a brother to me, and also later became the godfather to my kids. I am forever honored to have shared some of the most life-changing collaborations with him and will never forget the music we were able to make together.

I can wholeheartedly say that being a diligent worker is a large part of the reason that I have been able to do all that I am blessed to have done. I may not be able to control the exact opportunities I am presented with, but the part of the equation that I do have control over is whether or not I have prepared myself enough to accept whatever opportunities come my way. If I hadn't sharpened my arranging chops, I never would have been ready to accept *the* opportunity of a lifetime when I got that call from Frank. When you get the call, you won't have time to sit around and figure out if you can do it. If you prepare yourself in advance, you'll be able to accept whatever comes your way without even having to spend a second thinking about it.

For example, if you're going around telling people that you want to be a musician (or whatever profession you are pursuing) but you haven't practiced, you may be presented with an opportunity that you simply can't accept because you aren't ready. I've heard many people say they want to be a singer, but then when they're asked to sing on the spot, they shy away or can't remember the lyrics to a single song. You see, opportunities aren't usually hard to come by, but opportunities that you're properly prepared for are few and far between.

Also, when you do a job well once, there's almost no doubt that you'll get it again, or get referred to someone else. Everything in your life is a chain reaction, and your ability to deliver will usually be judged based on your last encounter. Can you imagine what would've happened if I'd completely blown my first chance at working with Lady Day? Or if I had repeated the same mistakes on my second gig with Bobby Tucker and Billy Eckstine? Or if I hadn't been ready for that first call from Frank in 1958? I wouldn't have lasted twenty minutes with him, let alone been called back again to work with him nearly six years later!

Good luck usually follows the collision of opportunity and preparation, so you've got to be prepared. Keep developing your skills, and then let whatever might happen, happen. It doesn't matter what job title you have, or if you feel as though the work you do is insignificant; do it to the best of your ability. Whether shining shoes, picking strawberries, setting bowling pins, or arranging for Frank, I carried the work ethic my father taught me into everything, and it has stuck with me to this very day. There will be plenty of moments in which the work you do goes unnoticed, but hear me when I say that someone is always watching. The fact that Bobby Tucker noticed my playing in the Bumps Blackwell Junior Band, and that Billy Eckstine remembered me enough to suggest my name to Nicole Barclay, are the perfect examples. Whatever you do, do it well, or not at all.

Most important, if you haven't learned to do well with what you have now, how can you ever expect to be entrusted with more? Laziness is no excuse, but if that *is* your excuse, I'd simply ask you to reassess your priorities. It's not enough to do the bare minimum if you expect to be the best at what you do. Odds are, if you are reading this, you *are* interested in learning how to take that next step, both personally and professionally. My advice to you is this: Always be ready to dive into the details, as it's the only way to ascend to the top of your field. And if you don't know where to start, hang around for the next Note because I've got a few ideas for you.

SHARPEN

YOUR

LEFT BRAIN

When I was starting to notate some of my earliest compositions and arrangements, I wrote a little note with an asterisk at the beginning that said, "Attention! Play all of the B notes a half-step lower because they sound funny if you play B natural." I was only thirteen years old then, and since I had never heard of a key signature, I had no idea that there was a symbol I could write at the beginning of the staff, which would achieve the same goal. Only after I started hanging around seasoned pros like Count Basie and the guys in the Lionel Hampton Band was I taught to just put a flat on the third line at the beginning so that I didn't have to write the note every single time. Discovering that there was a method showed me I had a lot to learn, and it confirmed that in order to become the best at what I set out to do, being emotionally invested in my music wasn't enough. Rather, I needed to understand the science behind my craft, or as I like to say, "Sharpen my left brain."

You see, there's a scientific theory that the right hemisphere of the brain is responsible for emotions and creativity, while the left hemisphere is responsible for intellect and analytics. But, for the sake of simplicity, I'll be referring to these two sections as the right and left brain. The emotional side (right brain) is said to be shaped and guided by our experiences and instincts, which come naturally, while the intellectual side (left brain) is said to be shaped and guided by science, as well as analytical and technical skills—which need to be practiced and honed. In a similar fashion, I'm convinced that music consists of two parts—soul and science—which are products of the right and left brain. On one hand, music is an expression of our emotions, but on the other hand, music is a science that is structured around the mathematical relationship between pitch and time (the study of music theory).

I learned the lesson of needing to sharpen my left brain through music, but after a whole lot of trial and error, I have found that the need to sharpen it can be applied to anything and everything in life. Whether you're a doctor or a carpenter or a chef, if you don't understand the ins and outs of your discipline, your passion will only get you so far. Because without taking the time to fine-tune your skills, your efforts will be built on a foundation that is bound to crumble once it is put to the test.

This discovery set me on a path of relentlessly trying to acquire knowledge that could support my growing desire to express my creativity, whether it be through music, film, production, you name it. Once I learned how to properly notate music, or sync music to picture when I began film scoring, or produce compelling live shows using scientific methods, I was able to take my artistry to the next level. Learning how to sharpen my left brain has been largely influential in how I've approached every creative endeavor, so allow me to tell you about how I've been able to do it, and how it has helped me gain credibility in my respective fields.

As I mentioned in Note A#, my appetite for knowledge started with reading Mr. Powe's books—from Glenn Miller on arranging, to Frank Skinner on film scoring—when I would go to his house to babysit his kids. Then, after I graduated from Garfield High School, I received a grant to study music at Seattle University. The courses eventually turned out to be a bit too boring, but instead of getting comfortable, I pursued more of a challenge and applied to Schillinger House (now known as Berklee College of Music). One semester later, I received a scholarship and transferred. It was at this school that I heard about the influential work of Nicolas Slonimsky, a Russian composer who studied and documented the mathematical components of music. His book, *Thesaurus of Scales and Melodic Patterns*, completely changed the game for me. I studied that thing inside and out and absorbed his insight on how there are absolutes in music and mathematics: absolutes that require a detailed understanding and practice. This book was like the Bible to music heads—I mean, even the legendary John Coltrane and the celebrated Charlie Parker (true pioneers of bebop) wouldn't leave home without it. Slonimsky's writing revealed a whole host of melodically plausible patterns, and it led me deeper into the science behind music theory. I couldn't get enough, and even after traditional schooling, I sought out as many opportunities as I could that would help me sharpen my left brain.

In 1955, at the age of twenty-two, the infamous leader of bebop Dizzy Gillespie called me up and said, "Young catter, I want you to play trumpet, arrange, and be musical director of my band. Put it together for me." The band in question was being sponsored by the United States State Department, to help bring cultural diplomacy abroad through jazz music, as summoned by the famous congressman from Harlem, Adam Clayton Powell Jr. However, one month before, George Avakian at Columbia Records had called me in for a job, working with and arranging for a uniquely gifted, unknown seventeen-year-old jazz singer and track star from San Francisco, that I'd already accepted. So I had a dilemma, but it only took me about a minute to decide. I went to George's office and said, "George, I really love your new singer, and I'm sorry, but I gotta serve my country," and I was off. Bebop was my everything, and I idolized Dizzy. Funny enough, the seventeen-year-old singer was Johnny Mathis, and he later went on to record "Chances Are" and "The Twelfth of Never" with Mitch Miller!

Anyway, while on the State Department tour, Dizzy and I were at a club in Buenos Aires after a gig and heard this cat playing jazz piano with a small combo. He introduced himself as

Lalo Schifrin; we came to find out he was a famous Argentinian pianist. After further conversation about our mutual interest in orchestration, he told me about Nadia Boulanger—one of the top teachers of twentieth-century composition—and that she would be able to teach me everything I wanted to know about composition, counterpoint, and orchestration. She was also the first female to conduct the New York Philharmonic and taught renowned figures like Leonard Bernstein, Michel Legrand, Aaron Copland, and Igor Stravinsky. I was dedicated to finding a way to study with her. My only barrier to entry was the fact that I had to audition, and her school was in France.

Well, fast forward to 1957, when I was back home living in New York and received the call to work for Barclay Records in Paris. The timing couldn't have worked out more perfectly. One of the first things I did after arriving was audition for Nadia. Much to my surprise, I landed a coveted spot in her class and began my quest to learn about orchestration. Back in the United States, I wasn't allowed to write for strings as a Black man, because strings were considered "too sophisticated" for people like me; so, learning how to write for strings with Nadia, and being able to simultaneously apply my newly acquired skills over at Barclay, was the knockout combo I needed.

As part of her classes, she had her students learn anything and everything about retrograde, inversion, counterpoint, and harmony by dissecting *L'Histoire du soldat*, *The Rite of Spring*, and various other Stravinsky compositions. She told us, "Until you find another note, learn what everybody has done with the twelve we have." It became an important point of development in my career, because delving into what experts had already done allowed me to make more advanced creative decisions, rather than having to start from scratch. She asserted that creating music requires structure, and that "the more restrictions you have, the more freedom you'll have." Although it might seem counterintuitive, unrestricted creativity usually leads to chaos because there is no strategy involved. Freedom is only realized within a well-defined structure; for example, *fortissimo* doesn't mean anything without *pianissimo*. Your music can't get loud if you don't start out soft, and vice versa. The interconnectedness of dynamics, tempo, and chord structure is how you create a masterpiece instead of a mess. This framework even applies to improvisation. Although improvisation is spontaneous, artists still need to rely on a fundamental knowledge of contrasting tempos in order to play a certain progression, while delicately balancing volume, and all other dynamics. As the great Pablo Picasso (who also happened to be my next-door neighbor for three years while I lived in the south of France with the Barclays; he resided in Villa La Californie with his wife Jacqueline, two goats, and three ducks!) established, "You've got to know the rules in order to break them." Music is a science that needs to be carefully studied.

I devoured the lessons she taught in class and spent even more time learning with her in private sessions, during which I'd simply listen as she talked about music for hours. I finally told her I wanted to learn about orchestration, and she agreed, but only under the condition that I'd take the first twenty-five bars of Ravel's *Daphnis et Chloé* and reduce the transposed score into a six-line concert-pitch sketch. It was a drill that taught me how to get everything in a symphony, plus percussion, on six lines, which became a necessary skill down the road when I dove into the world of film scoring. After bringing my finished piece to her, she replied: "Now transpose it up through all twelve steps." I didn't even know where to begin, but as I fumbled through her instructions, it was as if the trial by fire began to answer my own questions. Repeatedly studying and practicing the assignment (sharpening my left brain) provided me with the foundation I needed to become a great orchestrator, film composer, and over-all musician. That infrastructure was what helped pave the way for each subsequent phase of my career.

Years later, in 1964, when I was working as the vice president of A&R at Mercury Records back in New York, the founder, Irving Green, did a stock merger with Mercury Records and Philips, the multinational conglomerate company. Through the merger, Philips made me an offer of $1,000,000—more zeros than I had ever seen in my life—for a twenty-year contract. As much as I longed for financial security, I thought it over, and it broke down to a payout of about $50,000 a year for the next twenty years. Back in the day, $50,000 was a considerable salary, but I asked myself, "Is my life worth fifty grand a year?" I couldn't see it. I knew I still had much to learn about the entertainment industry as a whole. But, most important, I wanted to follow my dream of going to California to get into film scoring, which I'd previously gotten a taste of when I scored a small

Swedish film called *Pojken i trädet* in 1961. The film, translated as *The Boy in the Tree,* was written and directed by Oscar winner Arne Sucksdorff; I received the assignment after his daughter had seen my big band on a previous tour, tracked me down in a restaurant, and asked if I'd be the film composer.

Then, in 1964, famed director Sidney Lumet asked me to score a drama called *The Pawnbroker,* which turned out to be my first score for an American film. As grateful as I was for my role at Mercury Records, I couldn't see myself there for the rest of my career—especially after uncovering my passion for film scoring. So, I lined up a gig to score my first theme song, for an NBC show called *Hey Landlord,* and officially made the jump to California in 1965. Leaving Mercury turned out to be the best decision I ever made, because in total, I went on to compose more than fifty-one film and television scores.

Through the following years, I made sure to continue building upon the knowledge I had gained and to acquire new skills so that I could stay ahead of the curve. So, in an attempt to continue learning from the pros, I attended the author Robert McKee's highly acclaimed Story seminar in Los Angeles. It turned out to be some of the best thirty hours I've ever spent in my life. Over the course of this three-day event, McKee walked attendees through the substance, structure, style, and principles of storytelling, as it applies to marketing, filmmaking, and various other forms of communication. He outlined a strategy called "image systems," which is frequently utilized in filmmaking. And as he further clarifies in his book, *Story: Substance, Structure, Style, and the Principle of Screenwriting*:

An image system is a strategy of motifs, a category of imagery embedded in the film that repeats in sight and sound from beginning to end with persistence and great variation, but with equally great subtlety, as a subliminal communication to increase the depth and complexity of aesthetic emotion.

To demonstrate, he used the last ten hours of class to explain how films such as *Casablanca* and *Diabolique* use image systems. As we watched, he walked us through every scene and broke down recurrences of certain images or shapes that subliminally help set the tone for the viewer. More specifically, *Casablanca* uses an image system of "prisons." If you watch closely, you'll find frequent projections of prison bars, spotlights, striped clothing, and shadows of barbed wire present throughout the film in an effort to subconsciously reflect the theme of character imprisonment in the midst of a war.

Robert also guided us through a script dissection in which we discovered that nearly every three pages contain some type of joke, song, romantic moment, or conflict. Each component was purposefully placed so that the film was made up of 25 percent romance, 25 percent comedy, 25 percent music, and 25 percent conflict. This seminar was so pivotal to my understanding of film that I decided to attend it again, for another thirty hours. I returned again a few years later for a third round, and the more I learned about the ins and outs of every field within the entertainment industry, the more I began to understand how *every* profession has scientific components.

This made me think back to when I worked with an advertising agency on Madison Avenue in New York City where I learned that every single method of effective communication utilizes psychology. For example, the most powerful type of commercial is one that has a bass or baritone voiceover, paired with words written across the screen in big bold capitalized letters, so you simultaneously hear what you see. This was all done under the scientific reasoning that the subconscious mind typically retains 10 percent of what is heard and 30 percent of what is seen. So, when you pair audio and visual components, you've automatically secured 40 percent of the viewer's attention. It appeals to the subconscious mind: Without even realizing it, the viewer has subliminally received the message that the advertiser was intending to convey. Although it's no secret that advertisers make strategic decisions, it was simply mind-blowing to discover that there was a psychological component behind such decisions. The fact that creative choices were made in an effort to purposefully and psychologically impact a viewer further revealed to me that I needed to understand the entirety of my discipline in order to be an effective creator.

The most exciting part for me was when I got to apply the knowledge I acquired to my creations, because once I understood the science behind my craft, I was able to enhance my art. As I referred to earlier, you've got to know the rules in order to break them.

One of my favorite examples of this in action took place in 1996, when I produced the Oscars telecast at the Dorothy Chandler Pavilion in Los Angeles. Right before our host Whoopi

Goldberg announced the Sound Effects Editing category, I dedicated an entire segment to the importance of sound effects and how they can make a film come to life. To *show* how it was done, I had the percussionist Luke Cresswell along with Steve McNicholas, the co-founder of the dance percussion act Stomp, choreograph the dancers in a way that created live sound effects onstage that matched up with a silent film reel playing on screen in the background. For example, every time a door closed, a car honked, or some type of audible action should've happened on screen, the dancers' shoes, which were mic'd, created the sound effects. It was a beautifully choreographed piece that visually and audibly showed the audience the value of sound effects in filmmaking. In addition, for the announcement of the Best Original Song category, instead of having the presenters, Angela Bassett and Laurence Fishburne, read the list of nominees, I had them introduce the a cappella group Take 6 to *sing* the list of nominees in the form of an original song, instead of listing them off one by one.

And it didn't stop there. I had seven foot, two inch Kareem Abdul Jabbar and five foot, nine-inch Jackie Chan come out to present the awards for Best Short Film—the height difference between the two presenters was a visual reinforcement of the category. It also allowed for a bit of comic relief, as Kareem and Jackie emphasized their height difference throughout the segment. Kareem had to bend down to reach the microphone that was appropriately adjusted for Jackie, and man, it was hilarious. Everything—from Stomp, to Take 6, to Kareem and Jackie—was a purposeful blend of soul and science.

More recently, as shown in my Netflix documentary, *QUINCY*, I was asked to produce the 2016 opening ceremony for the Smithsonian National Museum of African American History and Culture in Washington, D.C. One of my favorite moments of the show was at the 37:15 mark when Tom Hanks introduced a segment about the Tuskegee Airmen display in the museum. Instead of simply playing a slideshow of the memorabilia that the museum had on display, we had Tom recite a beautifully written tribute about the history of the Airmen, and then we surprised the audience with an onstage appearance from seven surviving members. As they walked out on stage to "America the Beautiful" being sung by the West Point Glee Club, we also had the late General Colin Powell come out to shake hands with each member of the Tuskegee unit. It was an incredibly powerful moment and there wasn't a dry eye in that theater. Even after we re-aired it in 2020 on ABC, as a hopeful response to the civil unrest that unfolded over the summer, much of the public acclaim was centered around the emotionally charged Tuskegee Airmen segment.

Every single detail of that event was carefully planned so that the overall impact was rooted in true emotion. Although the history of the museum was the focal point, the goal was to inspire audience members by methodically piecing together a story that served to uplift. I worked on that production for over a year with my co-producer Don Mischer, along with our internal teams. We can *all* attest to the fact that every transition, story crescendo, and set design was purposefully created and placed.

Having done this time and time again, I'm tellin' you: If you want to create art that invades the subconscious mind and leaves a long-lasting impact, you've got to have the proper blend of soul and science. You've gotta do it right!

As a film scorer, I've set out to study nearly every element of filmmaking and scoring so that my left brain is properly prepared for any task. Scoring is a multifaceted process, consisting of an abstract combination of soul and science. The psychology behind scoring is totally subjective and extremely personal, but the process of synchronization, matching the music to the film, is all science. That's the part I had to (and still) study.

As a producer, I have to be able to take charge of virtually every phase of the creative process. From inception, to execution, to completion. Furthermore, if you want to have the kind of confidence you'll need as a producer in the studio, you must be proficient in your core musical skills, in addition to being able to handle all of the organizational and relational demands.

This lesson can apply to any and every position you assume, and I promise that what you learn in one field will often cross over to another. Similar to physical exercise, the process of sharpening your left brain may be frustrating at times, but it functions like a muscle that builds strength over time. As with anything, the more you sharpen that left brain of yours, the easier your tasks will become. I promise it's the most efficient way to excel in anything you attempt. Purposeful practice only leads to improvement, and you simply can't have one without the other.

This always makes me think back to when Alicia Keys was a young girl, and her mother asked me to give her some advice on how to become a singer. I told her to burn a CD composed of her top fifteen favorite artists and sing along to it over and over until she felt that she got all the notes and nuances down. I told her to do that because studying and practicing with the pros gives you a sense of what it's like to be a great singer before actually having to hit the stage. If you can keep up with the likes of Aretha Franklin and Whitney Houston, you can keep up with anyone. And, judging by the level of success that Alicia has realized today, she has undoubtedly sharpened that left brain of hers!

When you think about the role of the human brain, it's as if we've been given a computer that we can either choose to load with software and enhance the operation of, or leave sitting idle. It's completely up to you how you use it, but the sooner you acknowledge that the quality of your output is directly proportional to the input of your effort, the closer you will be to unlocking your fullest creative potential.

Nowadays, you'll never catch me leaving my house without a book of Sudoku and crossword puzzles, because actively solving them every day helps to keep my mind sharp. Man, everyone around me knows I'm a sucker for some puzzles! After all, as the old adage goes, "Use it or lose it."

All that is to say, if you want to be a great musician, learn the science behind how music works and never stop building on it. Learn about harmony, counterpoint, leitmotifs (a recurrent theme throughout a musical or literary composition associated with a particular person, idea, or situation), the construction of melody, and definitely orchestration. If it has anything to do with music, learn it! Soak up everything you possibly can about the type of music you're interested in pursuing, as well as every other kind. It's all connected. In the same way, if your goal is to become the world's best baker, learn what everyone else has done with the ingredients you're working with, and understand how every element works together to create a final product. The ways in which ingredients interact with each other are a science, and in order to bake freely, you need to understand what does and does not mix well.

Always remember that there's freedom within restriction. You've got to know the rules in order to break them. At my age, I'm always prepared to mix science with soul, but that's only because I've put in the work to achieve that balance. You can't expect it to happen overnight, and if you want to be an expert, you've got to know your stuff—360 degrees, 365 days a year. So, whether you're a film composer, an aspiring executive, or still figuring it out, I want to challenge you to delve deeper into learning the science behind your craft because I guarantee it will change the way you create. Knowledge never harmed anybody, and I know it ain't about to start today! So, hear me when I say, sharpen your left brain!

AVOID

PARALYSIS

FROM

ANALYSIS

NOTE

D#

I know we just talked a lot about the importance of sharpening your left brain, but don't get it twisted: There still needs to be a balance of science *and* soul. Otherwise, you may fall into the trap of paralysis from analysis. In other words, you may get so caught up in your own thoughts, or logistics thereof, that you wind up suffocating your artistry. Now, I know I'm not the only one who has ever hit a wall when it comes to writing music or creating, but the only thing that really matters in this business is how quickly you can get "unstuck." I believe one of the main reasons I've been fortunate enough to have had such a lasting career is the fact that I've learned how to get out of my own way.

There's no single formula for creativity, but if I had to choose one, this would be it. I'm telling you right now, learning this lesson might just be the difference between you landing or losing your next gig.

Getting out of your own way may seem like an abstract concept, but I promise it's simpler than you think. It's about first getting into a position that allows you to create freely, without internal judgment. For example, when I started scoring films, the toughest parts of the creative process were spent trying to scrape away all of the unnecessary thoughts running around in my head—from internal feelings of unworthiness to external voices that verbally told me I wasn't good enough. I had to keep chipping away at all of those thoughts until there was absolutely nothing left but the truth—that is, my soul and the message it wanted to communicate. Having tried it myself, I don't think you can write or create anything worthwhile if you suppress your instincts and emotions. You've got to be sitting deep in truth in order to create truth.

I've learned how to navigate the process of getting out of my own way through a variety of methods, but I've distilled them into four points which I hope will be helpful as you try to wade through your creativity and learn how to do the same. It pretty much comes down to:

1. Not putting yourself in a box
2. Listening to your gut instincts
3. The Goosebump Test
4. A great song and story

To jump right in, don't put yourself in a box; there's really no other way to put it. Without a doubt, I know that I never would have realized my dreams of becoming a producer, composer, artist, arranger, conductor, instrumentalist, record company executive, television station owner, magazine founder, multimedia entrepreneur, humanitarian, and, most important, father, if I allowed myself to be boxed in to what society expected of me. According to statistics, I should have only achieved *one* of those titles, or not even made it past my teenage years, based on the unfavorable environment I was born into. In fact, the older you get, the more restrictions society will try to impose on you; but, the more you allow yourself to grow, the more you will push right past those barriers.

As I discovered from my beloved brother-from-another-mother Ray Charles, the same rule applies to creativity. When I was fourteen and he was sixteen, he taught me how to read music in Braille and repeatedly told me, "Be pure and faithful to every genre of music," so that's what I did. I grew up respecting all types of styles and didn't allow classifications to limit what I could play. Ray and I never wrote music with a specific category in mind; we simply let our hearts make whatever type of music we wanted, with no regard for what we were expected to play as jazz musicians. From rock and roll, to rhythm and blues, to bebop, to pop, to hip-hop—we viewed labels as a way to classify the end product, not our creative process. This served me well in my later years, because when industry folks started making comments that I was a "sellout" and traded in my jazz chops for pop records, I had to laugh, because little did they know, I had been well-versed in all kinds of music (including gigs I used to play at bar mitzvahs and clubs all over town) since I was a kid. All I could say was, "You better have something to sell and know how to sell it!"

In 1973, I had the honor of producing *Duke Ellington . . . We Love You Madly*, a CBS TV special (my first television credit as a producer) that I organized for one of my jazz idols, Duke Ellington. It featured the likes of Aretha Franklin, Ray Charles, Sammy Davis Jr., Roberta Flack, and Count Basie. This show was the embodiment of Duke's philosophy that "there are only two kinds of music: good music and the other kind." After we wrapped, Duke gave me what would become one of my most prized possessions: a signed photograph with the inscription "To Q, who will be the one to de-categorize American music." I took it to heart and ever since have tried to do just that. This mentality has been integral to my creative success because attempting to close the gaps between genres has allowed me to defy what is traditionally possible. I've never stayed within a single lane. Instead, as soon as I reach the end of one, I hop right on over to the next. I've tried my best to encourage musicians to do the same by inviting them to collaborate with other artists they would normally never think to work with. You can hear examples of this cross-genre sound on my 1989 album, *Back on the Block*, when I had jazz queens like Sarah Vaughan and Ella Fitzgerald perform with rappers such as Ice-T, Kool Moe Dee, and Melle Mel. I've also done the same with just about every other project I've worked on.

I feel as though the charge that Ray and Duke gave me—to help dismantle genre classifications—has been woven into the very fabric of my calling. One of my latest attempts to do so was through the 2017 formation of my Subscription Video on Demand (SVoD) platform, Qwest TV: a place for music lovers of all genres to discover unexpected musical worlds. Each channel was designed to guide viewers through music, rather than genres, in unique ways to help expand the listeners' horizons. It's simply about sharing the good stuff and making it more accessible to each and every heart and soul across the globe.

In order for music to naturally evolve, it's important for critics to stop separating musicians based on their "type" and simply assess music at face value. Otherwise, this hyperclassification prevents musicians from exploring their full potential because they get stuck in a routine of creating with bowling bumpers on. They've been told so often to stay in their lane that they never even think of exploring other facets of their field. Simultaneously, artists need to take their art into their own hands and not allow man-made restrictions to dictate their future. I was fortunate enough to learn at the very beginning of my career that not only is it OK to play all kinds of music, but it should also be a driving force.

I am certain that maintaining a broad perspective on my musical, as well as personal, capabilities has played an important role in my accomplishments. It has allowed me to tap into every single one of my creative reserves. Most important, it prevented me from placing a cap on my potential and, therefore, getting in my own way.

So, don't restrict yourself, and especially don't allow others to do it for you.

The second practice that has also greatly helped me to avoid falling prey to paralysis from analysis has been listening to my gut instincts.

When asked, "How are we to regard our instincts?" I turn to the author Malcolm Gladwell. He explained it best when he said, "Well, we ought to take them seriously. They can be really good, or they can be terrible and mislead us horribly. But in both cases, we have an obligation to take them seriously and to acknowledge they are playing a role. The mistake is to dismiss them." And in his brilliant book *Blink* he further asserts that "insight is not a lightbulb that goes off inside our heads. It is a flickering candle that can easily be snuffed out." It's the perfect analogy because we so often dismiss our greatest ideas, thinking they're supposed to make some type of grand entrance when, in reality, they may often just present themselves in the form of a whisper. This is why it is essential to quiet your conscious mind and, instead, tap into your subconscious mind—the part that guides your intuition and ability to hear those whispers.

It has been scientifically stated that humans either operate in "alpha" or "beta" mental states when awake, meaning that our brains are either in a state of calm or rest (alpha) or highly active (beta). Knowing this, I've decided that I don't believe in writer's block. It's not a block; rather, it's the need to move into an alpha state so you can hear what your heart is trying to tell you. Only then can you quiet your conscious mind and tap into your subconscious, which helps you think more clearly without internal judgment. Have you ever wondered why children speak their minds with no inhibition? It's because their brain waves are at an alpha frequency!

The composer Leonard Bernstein, a longtime friend of mine, told me that he and his writing partner Stephen Sondheim wrote the classic musical *West Side Story* completely in an alpha state. He would lie on the couch, prop one leg over the side, and relax until reaching the point between being awake and falling asleep. That's when he wrote the music. Having tried it myself, I can confirm that this practice works. Whenever I need to write a significant amount of music or just need to get unstuck, I'll lie down with my back on the floor, legs up on the bed, and have my music pad and pencil ready to go. After I've relaxed just enough and find myself slipping into an alpha state, I'll write whatever comes to me.

There's a lot of research out there that presents various ways for entering into an alpha state of mind, but all I know is that I don't create music any other way. Knowing how powerful it is, I can't help it! I've heard fellow collaborators say, "Quincy just sits there with his head in his hands while in the studio," but little do they know that it's because I'm deep in my creative process. Also, whenever I'm producing for other artists, I make sure to schedule our sessions late in the night when the musicians are getting sleepy, just so they can't overthink when recording their parts. Without fail, and often without even recognizing it, they deliver their best performances right as they begin to slip into an alpha state.

Alfred Newman used to say that you should always "keep your score paper and pen right near you, 'cause if you're not up, God will take it down the street to (Henry) Mancini!" So, whenever you hear that whisper, you better listen and write it down. I'll never forget one time I fell asleep after writing in an alpha state. When I woke up about four hours later, I looked at my paper and had already written about ten pages! Learning this method of creation largely influenced my ability to turn out so much music because I didn't allow myself to block what was naturally coming through me. I believe we are a terminal for a higher power, and that your creativity comes through you, not solely from you. Regardless of individual beliefs, if we're not keeping ourselves open to what is being transmitted through us, then we risk missing the whispers.

And as I learned from two of my mentors, the composers Victor Young and Alfred Newman, it's important to "just write and turn the page. Never look back." This proved to be an important aspect of creating in an alpha state, because it's essential that you don't block what your subconscious mind is trying to tell you. Sometimes it's difficult to get started, but you've got to stop overthinking and just begin, even if it's only a single word or shape. Before I pursued music, I explored various art forms such as drawing and painting, and I would always start with a charcoal sketch. Even if I didn't know what I wanted the end product to look like, I just put down a basic structure or contour. Then from there, I'd add watercolors and finally oil. When I started producing music, I used a similar process. That is, I tried not to get locked in right away with an expectation of a final product. Instead, I followed my instincts and translated them into a basic shape or sound. Then, I built on top of it by defining dynamics, colors, density, and so on. Start with an image or melody, and let it out. And as the sketch or song takes shape, you can lay on the watercolors.

Creativity is informed by what you feel, not what you think, and learning to tune into those feelings is what is ultimately going to carry you through when distractions come. I've 100 percent relied on my instincts throughout my career; without doing so, I know I wouldn't have been able to create art that has stood the test of time. I recognize that it's easier said than done, but the next method I'm going to share with you is without a doubt the best way to do it.

And that method is "the Goosebump Test."

If the music I'm creating gives me goosebumps, odds are it'll do the same for at least one other person on this planet. But if it doesn't move me at all, and I'm trying to do it for the sake of getting a reaction out of someone else, I'll get stuck in a never-ending cycle of mediocrity. It doesn't work. On every project I've done, from the highest-selling to the least, I simply started with a desire to make the best music possible—music that touches the soul and mind. Music, and art as a whole, is a strange beast. You can't see it, taste it, touch it, or smell it, but you sure can feel it. I can never predict the outcome, or how people will react, but I can tell when a piece of music gives me goosebumps.

Getting locked into making a product that you *think* the public will want only robs you of authenticity. I can't start a project if I'm focused on what critics will say or what listeners might think because that type of attitude only serves to override my natural instincts, which is a much more powerful and direct source of inspiration.

This is not to be mixed up with acts of collaboration or receiving feedback, which are helpful tools. Rather, I'm talking about when you allow external opinions to permeate your creative process before you even get started; that's how you wind up ignoring the Goosebump Test.

I swear by this assessment because I get goosebumps every time something really touches me: music, movies, poetry, all of it. If I don't feel it, then there's nothing to talk about. I believe I acquired this skill having started out in the world of jazz, because jazz is born out of improvisation. It's a fast-paced art form that demands you to create on the spot, leaving no room for second guessing. And it's completely built around feeling. This foundation served me well because I've created some of my best work on a time crunch. Remember "Soul Bossa Nova" from Note C? You know, the track that became the theme song for the *Austin Powers* franchise? I wrote that in twenty minutes.

Having endless amounts of time to work on a project is a luxury, but it can also be a breeding ground for paralysis from analysis because you allow yourself to overthink. Going straight for the goosebumps will save you time in the long run because it prevents you from trying to force your art into something it's not supposed to be. If you don't feel it, I promise you that no one else will either.

In a similar vein, it's easy to get caught up in what we think other people will want. Along the way, we wind up forgetting the most important ingredients in learning how to get out of your own way: a great song and story. I can attest to the fact that this fourth and final method has saved me from wasting time on trying to fix what simply can't be repaired.

Let's break it down. A great song can make the worst singer in the world a star, but a bad song can't be saved by the three greatest singers on the planet. If you don't have a great song or a great story, then there's no need to even spend your time on it.

With the technology that we now have, it's easier than ever for artists to embellish tracks or specifically engineer them for the sake of virality, but timeless songs are just that: timeless. It doesn't really matter what kind of loops, beats, rhymes, or hooks you try to add because, at its core, it's still just a bad song. But what makes a piece of music so special that it can outlive the singer who brought it to life? What makes a song an anthem? There is no one way to create a great song because if there was, everyone would be doing it. Great songs do have identifiable characteristics and qualities, though, with the common denominator being connection. Pure connection.

One of my favorite examples of this is Lesley Gore's 1964 single, "You Don't Own Me," which I had the honor of sourcing and producing for her when I was working at Mercury Records. It peaked at number two on the Billboard charts, but I couldn't be angry that it didn't reach number one because it was right behind the Beatles' first American hit, "I Want to Hold Your Hand." "You Don't Own Me" spent thirteen weeks on the Billboard Hot 100 Chart and has since become an unspoken anthem for female empowerment. I never could have imagined the sort of life the track would wind up living, but from the start it gave us goosebumps.

Lyrically, it holds an incredibly powerful and relatable message that has transcended racial borders, traditional gender roles, and the typical life cycle of a song. If you take a look at a few lines below, there are no questions posed—only declarative statements.

You don't own me
I'm not just one of your many toys
You don't own me
Don't say I can't go with other boys

It wasn't written to ask for permission, as so many songs that were penned for females had previously done. Rather, it was a pivotal collaboration amongst Lesley, a seventeen-year-old who was beginning to come into her own as a female adult, and two songwriters, David White and John Madara, who were rightfully outraged by the misogynistic messaging that was perpetuated in the industry. David and John have gone on record to say that they "were disgusted by how much music written for female singers in the early 1960s centered on mooning over guys and decided to write a song about a woman telling a guy off." Madara also pointed out that the song was shaped by his upbringing in a multiracial neighborhood in Philadelphia, as well as his participation in the civil rights movement. Instead of forcing the song to fit into what was traditionally acceptable for a female to sing, they tapped into an essential part of humanity: the desire to be treated equally. Although it was tailored to a female perspective, the lyrics as a whole created enough versatility for it to mold to virtually any listener. It was written as a declaration of independence, birthed out of a deep sense of emotion, and stimulates that same sense of feeling within the listener.

Sonically, it starts in a minor key, but transitions into a major key along with the chorus. Everything you hear reflects what Lesley is saying: The intensity of the verse's lyrics is supported by the choice of chords, and then as she leaps into words of victory and authority in the chorus, the music echoes that same feeling. A great song has elements of surprise, inspiration, and momentum, and the movement of the chords, in unison with the lyrics, does exactly that. The ear quickly gets used to a sound when it remains static, so if you don't switch it up, the ear goes to sleep. There's a sense of thematic unity that appeals to the subconscious mind, and takes the listener on a sonically and lyrically exciting journey.

The timing of the release of the track was also essential, due to the correlation of the lyrics to the overarching message of the women's rights movement that was bubbling up in the '60s and into the '70s, as well as the ongoing civil rights movement of the '50s and '60s. The song began to assume a life of its own, from radio play, to word of mouth, to street rallies, and beyond; everywhere I turned, the song was being adopted as an anthem for female empowerment, and for anybody who simply wanted to proclaim, "Don't tell me what to do. Don't tell me what to say."

And it didn't stop in the '60s.

In 2015, my co-producer Parker Ighile and I re-recorded the track with an up-and-coming artist named Grace. It was a modern take on the song, featuring G-Eazy, that went platinum in 2016, and became the trailer song for DC's *Suicide Squad*. At the time of this writing, the song has generated more than one billion streams across digital service providers. It was a beautiful, full-circle moment because Grace, like Lesley, was also seventeen when we recorded her version. I felt that the song's message was one that should be reiterated for this new generation, and it worked.

From becoming an empowering female anthem during the time of the women's rights movement in the '60s and '70s, to then taking on a life of its own during the height of the #MeToo movement, the song remained relevant due to its ability to connect. Even during the years between the 1963 and 2015 recordings, the song morphed into a representative for various causes, because at the end of the day, it carried a powerful message and connected to movements greater than the experience of any one individual. It became the theme song that Goldie Hawn, Diane Keaton, and Bette Midler sang in the iconic divorcee scene in the 1996 comedy *The First Wives Club*. And, in 2018, as an homage to this scene and the empowering message behind "You Don't Own Me," Ariana Grande debuted her hit single, "thank u, next" on *The Ellen DeGeneres Show*, with an interpretation of that exact same performance from *The First Wives Club*. Also in 2018, the all-female cast of *Saturday Night Live* did their own rendition of the song with actress Jessica Chastain on the night of the Women's March. Time and again, it connected with listeners, regardless of race, gender, or generation, and proved that it didn't matter *when* the song was written—it was just as important and relevant nearly fifty years later.

Regardless of any re-recordings or new production we added to the track, the bottom line is that the song itself possesses undeniable characteristics and qualities that have made it memorable and impactful. That's really what it comes down to. You can try to ideate all day long about what you want to add to your art, but if it doesn't have a solid foundation on its own then you're bound to create on sinking sand. Forcing yourself to create a product that you *think* people want rather than letting it flow from a place of truth, only prevents you from achieving true connection with your audience.

So, regardless of what you are told or think you should be, never put yourself in a box, listen to your gut instincts and lean into the whispers, always go for the goosebumps, and strip everything down until you know you've got a great song or story. In short, move out of your way so that you can make way for what is to come naturally. I've abided by these rules since the beginning stages of my career, and I will continue to abide by them for as long as I live and create on this planet. Getting into a flow without giving your conscious mind a second to project internal judgments is the sweet spot, so even if a word or phrase doesn't make sense in the moment, write it down! You are often your own biggest creative block, so stop monitoring yourself and let. It. *Flow!*

THE POWER

OF BEING

UNDER-

ESTIMATED

NOTE

E

I hope that Note D# was helpful to your creative process; however, we didn't quite cover all of the landmines to watch out for when learning how to create freely. In fact, there is another major component that isn't always within your control: the opinions of others. Naysayers have repeatedly told me that I wasn't good enough or smart enough to achieve my goals, but I'm fortunate to have learned the power of being underestimated. If people overestimate you, they get in your way, but if they underestimate you, they get out. For example, if people place high expectations on you, the pressure of trying to avoid failure can become a significant distraction to your progress. If there are no, or low, expectations placed on you, then you have the freedom to create without scrutiny. Once I got over being told I was unqualified or unworthy, the doubtful feeling that I wasn't good enough ultimately became the fuel that propelled me forward. Finding myself in this position, more times than I can count, has been partially responsible for my successes.

Instead of being seen as a threat to powerful players in the industry, I was often viewed as nothing more than an underdog who didn't stand a chance at achieving commercial success. Being underestimated is the best position to be in because it provides you with an opportunity to not only meet expectations, but also to exceed them. Learning this lesson has been invaluable in my career because instead of thinking I've been set up to fall short, I view it as though I've been uniquely positioned to surpass the bars that have been set for me. After all, I know we've all witnessed at some point or another that the pressure of being overestimated too early in one's career can be detrimental if the artist is not properly prepared. Think about it. Have you ever wondered why one-hit wonders are called one-hit wonders? With extraordinarily high expectations placed on an artist after an initial release, some individuals aren't ever able to follow up with equal or greater content. It's always better to build from the ground up than to try and catch up.

Most important, being underestimated helps to keep the ego in check. Being prematurely hyped up and congratulated can lead to arrogance. Getting a big head doesn't do anything for you except make you look like a fool.

And for all the same reasons, you should never over-promise and under deliver. It's always better to surprise your critics than to prove them right. Don't walk around boasting that you're the "best" because your work will speak for itself. Instead of chasing fame, lean into your time of obscurity, or position of unexpected greatness, to plan and prepare for your next endeavor. The time of least attention is often when you can see the most clearly, without having the opinions of others as a distraction.

Regardless, you can't allow other people's expectations of you to overshadow who you really are. Placing too much emphasis on the assumptions of others is the quickest way to fail because expecting validation from external sources will only leave you feeling empty. It's a meaningless pursuit. You'd think that after achieving a certain level of success, negative speculations would dissipate, but I can say from experience that they only intensify. I've been underestimated for being too young, and I've been underestimated for being too old. It's a never-ending cycle, so, it's ultimately up to you to figure out if you will settle into living the life that you are *expected* to live or the life that you are *meant* to live.

There are numerous instances in which I've found power in being underestimated, but one of the most ironic memories is from when I began working with Michael Jackson as the producer of his top three albums, *Off the Wall*, *Thriller*, and *Bad*. Music history might look a bit different if I allowed negative opinions to stand in the way of what I knew I was capable of.

But as I said, prematurely boasting only sets you up to look like a fool, so I'll let you decide what you want to take from the following anecdote.

By the late '60s, I was getting completely burned out from doing movie scores. I had done thirty-five of them and had both hits and flops. Most composers do one or two a year, but I never did fewer than that. I once did eight! I was moving at an unsustainable pace. I remember often sleeping only three hours a day and running cold water over my wrists to stay awake. I also had three more kids after Jolie at this point, including Rachel, Tina, and Quincy Jones III, so there weren't many hours to work with in the day. Simultaneously, film scorers (especially Black film scorers) were at the bottom of the Hollywood food chain, and easily replaceable. It felt as though my value in the industry was constantly hanging by a thread. At the drop of a dime, I could be cut loose. Most important, I wanted to get away from the rigidity of having to write music to pictures. I longed to get back into the record business and wanted to make albums under my own name, produce for other artists, and facilitate a more free-flowing creative process. I didn't want to think about any deadlines. I simply wanted to create what gave me goosebumps.

In 1969, I signed a deal with Creed Taylor's Impulse! Records, which was distributed by A&M, and did a good number of albums through the '70s, including *Walking in Space*, one of the first jazz-fusion records, *Gula Matari, Body Heat*, a whole host of projects with The Brothers Johnson, and many more. Toward the end of the '70s, I was recruited back to film after Sidney Lumet asked me to be the music producer and supervisor for his new movie, *The Wiz*. I didn't want to do it, but since Sidney helped me get my first scoring assignment, on *The Pawnbroker* back in 1964, I couldn't say no.

I had previously met Michael Jackson when he was only twelve years old, but *The Wiz* brought us together for our first official collaboration, since he was cast in the role of Scarecrow. When we began rehearsals, Michael was getting ready to do his own album on Epic Records and he asked me to help him find a producer. My plate was pretty full trying to get pre-production for *The Wiz* going, so I couldn't even think about it at the time. But over the course of our rehearsals, I came to see that, on top of his otherworldly talents, Michael had a work ethic like I'd never seen before. No matter what, he was always prepared. He ensured that every dance step, line, and lyric was perfected to a T, and even memorized the lines of his co-stars.

In one scene, he was instructed to pull little pieces of paper out of his straw chest. They were filled with proverbs from famous philosophers and he kept mispronouncing Socrates. After three days of mispronouncing his name as "*Sow*-cray-tees," and receiving no correction, I pulled him aside during a break and whispered, "Michael, before it becomes a habit, I think you should know that the name is pronounced '*Sock*-ra-tees.'"

With the utmost humility, he said, "Really?"

Without even taking a second to think about it, I replied with, "I'd like to take a shot at producing your new record." His ability to take critique, on top of his work ethic and talent, indicated that he was exactly the kind of artist I would want to work with. He agreed.

Later, when Michael approached his label, Epic Records, about having me produce the album, his A&R reps told him, "No way. Quincy's too jazzy. He's only done The Brothers Johnson. He's a jazz arranger and composer."

It was the same type of response that I'd heard repeatedly over the years. They didn't know about the extent of my musical background, and they told Michael that Kenny Gamble and Leon Huff should do it. He eventually marched back to Epic with his managers, Freddy DeMann and Ron Weisner, and demanded that I produce his record. Much to his label's dismay, they agreed, but didn't expect much from me. And although they agreed, there wasn't a whole lot of cooperation. At that point it didn't matter though, because the ball was left in my court. I knew that I could either meet their low expectations or exceed them. In addition to their doubts about the level of my competency, many also wondered if Michael could make it as a solo artist in his adult years without the support of his brothers.

I had of course known about his Jackson 5 days, but I was interested in helping him break out of that former persona he was locked into. I wanted to push him beyond just dance music and see how far he could stretch his musicality. I had recently seen him at the Oscars singing "Ben," a song about a rat (for the film, *Ben*), which I knew wasn't going to cut it.

More than anything, I wanted to help him with his artistic development and get him to dig deeper, with no limitations on how far he could go musically. He had all the talent and drive. He did his homework. He just needed some guidance. I tested his creativity from every angle and applied everything I'd learned over the years to help him with his artistic growth, like dropping keys a minor third to give him flexibility and a more mature range in his upper and lower registers. I played around with tempo changes. I wanted to make a pop album that blended elements of R&B, disco rhythms, top-of-the-line arrangements, and, of course, his vocals. I gathered what I called my "Killer Q Posse," which consisted of Rod Temperton, one of the best songwriters to have ever lived on this planet; Bruce Swedien, the engineer of all engineers; Greg Phillinganes, a virtuosic keyboardist; Jerry Hey, a monster trumpeter and arranger; Louis Johnson, the youngest of The Brothers Johnson; John "J. R." Robinson, a fellow Berklee alum and the drummer for Rufus; Paulinho Da Costa from Brazil on percussion; and many other great musical talents.

Although it was impossible to predict the record's chances of success, we collectively poured 110 percent into every track and nuance of the album. In an attempt to steer Michael toward songs with more depth and emotion than he had ever sung before, I got Stevie Wonder's "I Can't Help It," Paul McCartney's "Girlfriend," Tom Bahler's "She's Out of My Life" (a track that I was initially going to give to Frank Sinatra!), Rod Temperton's "Rock With You," and, of course, "Don't Stop 'Til You Get Enough." Michael did most of his vocals live, with no overdubs. The resulting record, *Off the Wall*, sold tens of millions of copies.

It became the biggest-selling Black record in history. How's that for being too "jazzy"? Ironically, Epic was about to do a round of layoffs, but *Off the Wall* saved the jobs of many of the doubters who previously claimed that "Quincy is the wrong guy." It also became the first album to generate four American

Top 10 hits. Due to the success of *Off the Wall*, Michael and I went on to record *Thriller* (which is, as of this writing, still the bestselling album of all time) and *Bad*.

The entire experience reinforced the fact that people are always going to have opinions about your qualifications. What really matters is what you do with them. Focusing too much on what others have to say about you will lead you down a path to defeat before you've even had a chance to act. You can either entertain their skepticism or remove the chains from your creativity by allowing yourself to rise to the occasion. I *still* have to remind myself of this lesson because my being underestimated didn't stop after *Off the Wall*, or *Thriller*, or *Bad*. In fact, the more ears that heard those albums, the more opinions I had coming at me.

But now, instead of being underestimated for my capabilities, I'm underestimated for my age. People often ask me when I'm going to retire, but my only response is, "I'm just starting. Retired? You take the 're' off of that and it's 'tired.' I'm not tired yet." If you never leave, you never have to make a comeback, and that's exactly what I plan on doing. There's nothing wrong with retiring, especially after you've put in decades of hard work, but it's just not for me. I'm not interested in letting my age dictate my competency. If anything, the older I get, the more I learn and want to apply myself to my work, my music, and my life.

I've continued to lean into being underestimated in just about every business endeavor because it has placed me and my team at Quincy Jones Productions (QJP) in a position of least resistance. For example, we manage a roster of talented artists—the best of the best, in my opinion—but we've been told countless times that some of our artists are too "jazzy," or not "well-known enough" to receive certain opportunities. Well, let me tell you right now: As of this writing, one of our artists, Jacob Collier, has won five Grammy® Awards and has been nominated for nine, including Album of the Year. How's that for being too jazzy? I'm tellin' you, these kids are *it*. Alfredo Rodríguez, ASHER YELO, Dirty Loops, Eli Teplin, Erick the Architect, Jonah Nilsson, Justin Kauflin, Kanya, MARO, McClenney, Music Box, Richard Bona, Sheléa, Yeti Beats, and more. Every single one of them continues to kick butt wherever they go and in whatever they do. If you read their stories on my website, quincyjones.com, you'll see exactly what I mean. I'm extremely proud of these cats and proud to call them family because they all know what it means to put in the work. A requirement to be a part of our roster is to have the left *and* right brain down, and they've all got it.

Also under our QJP umbrella, we have cultivated several promising products and partnerships, including my piano teaching technology company, Playground Sessions.

After connecting with the founder and CEO, Chris Vance, back in 2012, I helped co-create the company to help more people discover the joy of learning how to play the piano. For me, it's impossible to imagine a more positive application of technology than one that helps people everywhere experience the power of playing music on their own. Nearly 85 percent of people from around the world have a desire to learn. Unfortunately, the traditional approach to learning has failed most who have tried.

When approaching investors and discussing our vision for how technology, gamification, and big data could be combined to make learning more fun and accessible to the masses, we were faced with a lot of noes and closed doors. Many people doubted that we would ever be able to make a product fun and easy enough to achieve mass consumer product appeal.

Even teachers joined the "no train" and told us outright that students would not be able to successfully learn piano on their own at home.

Contrary to these early naysayers, Playground Sessions is now the number-one, industry-rated digital learning tool for piano. More than one billion notes have been played on our platform, and our students enjoy a success rate of more than 90 percent.

Not only has our team built some of the best technology, but we are also proud to say that we are using the app to help support piano teachers who have found that Playground is a great supplemental tool for their students, since it can keep them inspired between in-person lessons.

During the COVID-19 pandemic, when people couldn't leave their places of residence, nor socialize with family and friends, it's evident that the public widely turned to music. Instruments were flying off the shelves, almost as much as toilet paper, and Playground was ready to help thousands all around the world when it was needed most. It was a firsthand display of the healing power of music, and I'm extremely proud of my whole team at Playground Sessions because they've worked tirelessly to create a product that we're excited to share with the world.

Most important, through our app, we've given more than one hundred million lessons to people who want to learn to play the piano. Finding a piano in that rec center back in Seattle was what saved my life, and it makes my soul smile to be able to share the same gift of music with others.

On top of the software development, I've continued diversifying my efforts because, when you're underestimated in one area, your critics will never see you coming from the other side. It's all about strategically choosing the directions of your next pursuit. Just when I'm told I'm too old to produce, I hit 'em with a TV special. All joking aside, I'm fortunate to still be in a position to create and collaborate. In the past few years, my team and I have produced major events including *Taking the Stage: African American Music and Stories That Changed America*, the opening of the Smithsonian National Museum of African American History and Culture; The Broad Museum's *Soul of a Nation Celebration; Soundtrack of America,* the five-night celebration of the opening of The Shed in New York City's Hudson Yards, and many more. When we're not producing events, we're booking talent for my Q's Bar and Lounge venue in the Palazzo Versace Hotel in Dubai. And when we're not doing that, we're helping to develop artists, booking talent at the historic (and my favorite) Montreux Jazz Festival in Switzerland, creating new lines of consumer electronics with Harman and JBL, and making award-winning films, such as *Keep On Keepin' On* and

QUINCY. We're not called an "all-encompassing entertainment company" for nothing! Every decision is informed by a strategy.

Most important, I'm in the business of rooting for underdogs. Through our investment division, we became early investors in Spotify, back in 2011, as well as Alibaba, Wayfair, Uber, and many more. You've got to be able to see not only what's in front of you, but also what's around the corner.

This principle doesn't just apply to me. Take a look at Apple. Before they dominated the consumer electronics, software, and online services spaces, they were told numerous times that they would never make it in the industry.

I could go on all day with examples. Netflix? Forget about it. They could've been spotted from a mile away, but Blockbuster was so comfortable with their success in the industry that they didn't think anything of the fledgling company competing for market share. Blockbuster even had a chance to buy Netflix, but with an ego-driven ship, they laughed at Netflix's offer and grew complacent with their position in the industry. By 2010, Blockbuster was bankrupt, and Netflix completely took over the market. Slow and steady wins the race, but an ego will end it.

If you find yourself leaning more toward the side of a critic, rather than on the side of those who are criticized, never dismiss unlikely winners. However, if you do, be prepared to show up at their doorstep with an apology letter!

And if you find yourself on the side of those who have been criticized, as I often have, remember that you don't need to fight back with bitterness. Focus on your goals and what you know you are capable of, and that's all the revenge you need to take. Whether it's your skin color, age, a disability, or any number of things, people are always going to find something about you to diminish. It's inevitable.

But as for me, I will continue to make strides because I don't allow negative assessments of myself to inform who I am. At more than eighty-eight, I feel like I'm just getting started, regardless of how many times I'm told it's time to quit.

DO WHAT'S

NEVER

BEEN DONE

BEFORE

Having learned the power of being underestimated, I'm blessed to have been able to achieve more than I ever could have predicted and seen more sides of life than I ever could have expected. But, internalizing this lesson alone isn't the reason I can *still* say that I feel like I'm just getting started at eighty-eight years old. Rather, it's because I learned the significance of dreaming big. More specifically, I learned the importance of never fully catching up to my dreams, and maintaining sizable goals to help me achieve them. This has helped prevent me from developing an ego, because otherwise, if I were to have accomplished all of my aspirations by the time I was sixty, it would be easy to rest on my laurels. Since my dreams have always grown with my age, I know I'll always have something to strive for. Learning to place weight on my ambitions was an important lesson to learn because it's what has kept me motivated for such a long time and allowed me to do all that I've been able to.

I've definitely reached moments where I've wanted to throw in the towel, but knowing that I still have much to accomplish gives me a sense of excitement about what is to come. I never allow myself to get so comfortable with my past that I neglect the possibilities of my future. To me, settling isn't a neutral position; rather, its only charge is negative, because it's the equivalent of losing momentum in the middle of an upward climb. So, if I don't set audacious goals and stretch myself to try and achieve them, then I'll never know what I am capable of. As the saying goes, "You'll never get an A if you're always afraid of getting an F."

Our minds are limited, so we tend to place limitations on ourselves from the jump, but I've found beauty in the unknown by simply giving my mind the freedom to explore. Learning to keep myself stocked with oversize dreams is what has led me down endless roads of opportunities. Whenever I hear the phrase "That's never been done before," I feel like a lion being thrown some meat. It immediately piques my interest and points me in the direction of my next challenge. I never know what I'm going to find, but the more I push myself, the more I surprise myself. If I had been closed off to the possibilities from the start, then I would have failed before I even tried.

There wasn't *one* specific moment in which I learned the lesson of dreaming big, but the gradual accumulation of uncapped aspirations is what has allowed me to achieve things that I otherwise know I would not have been able to. In fact, it's what led me to become the first Black vice president of a major record label, the first Black nominee for a Best Original Song Academy Award, the first Black individual to be nominated twice in the same year for Best Song and Best Score Academy Award, the first Black conductor and music director of the Academy Awards ceremony, amongst many other "firsts." I don't say this to boast a list of accomplishments; if anything, being the first doesn't impress me because that often means *only*. It may be an indicator of progress—in my case, specifically for the Black community—but it's not a sign of being *there* yet. That's still a problem. With that said, achieving these accomplishments is not about me as an individual; rather, it's about using my gifts and talents to help add to the collective.

When we allow ourselves to dream, the possibilities are endless for the whole. For example, when I think about Martin Luther King Jr.'s dream—that every individual would be afforded equal rights—I can't help but think how the dreams of one are inextricably linked to the dreams of another. Without MLK's hope for the collective, we may not have given ourselves the personal liberties to believe it as individuals. I didn't always view myself as someone who would be deemed a changemaker, but that's exactly the point: It's easy to look at others and justify why they *can* and you *can't*. One person in particular who really knew how to break down such mental barriers was the great Nelson Mandela. I was honored to have spent many years with him and even had the opportunity to take part in the American delegation at his inauguration in South Africa. One of the things he repeatedly reminded me of was the concept of Ubuntu, a word that derives from the Zulu phrase *"Umuntu ngumuntu ngabantu,"* which basically means the collective is always greater than the individual. As I previously mentioned, it's not about "I, Me & Mine"; it's about "We, Us & Ours." When we seek to create change on a singular level, we ultimately create change for others beyond ourselves.

For example, as I've moved forward in pursuit of excellence, regardless of the task, I am honored to have broken many barriers and records. I really only say this because it ties back to what I told you in Note C: This world needs your gifts and talents. If you don't step up to the plate, then who will? Giving yourself the permission to dream and do what's never been done before gives others permission to do the same. Think about it: Haven't you ever looked at someone you admire and thought to yourself, "Well, she or he was the first person to break that record, so I can do it too"? When you get the chance to open doors that have traditionally been slammed shut, it's important that you hold the door open for the next person to walk through. It's not about feeding your ego with a list of accolades; it's about continuing to pave the path that has been set before you.

In the early '80s, one of the doors that had yet to be fully opened was the one to the hip-hop world. Mainstream media continuously highlighted and glorified the violence surrounding the music, but neglected to showcase how hip-hop was one of the most remarkable celebrations of Black culture and life. I was a tremendous believer and supporter of hip-hop and rap, and knew that you just couldn't group every single artist under the banner of "gangsta rap." There were so many incredible kids out there with brilliant minds being forced into a narrative when they were really just creating music as an expression of their everyday lives.

You see, I had been experimenting with various types of rapping techniques for a while. I had a growing interest in the (originally) African art form, and my 1975 album, *Mellow Madness*, came from that exploration. It incorporated poetic rap verses and lyrics arranged as call-and-response chants, which I formulated with funk rhythms and African percussion instruments. It also featured a rap called "Beautiful Black Girl," performed by the Watts Prophets, a group known for combining jazz music and spoken-word performance.

Then in 1977, I had the tremendous honor to score the landmark miniseries *Roots*, based on the legendary writer Alex Haley's original book. I threw myself into researching percussive and traditional songs, as well as a vast amount of African history. I set out to write a score that spoke to the experience of my native people and I recruited some of the best of the best South African musicians, such as Caiphus Semenya and Letta Mbulu. Scoring this project was deeply emotional, having dived deep into learning about the transatlantic slave trade and all of its aftereffects. Uncovering knowledge about my roots, my people, and my music was a transformative experience, and ultimately it's what led me to have a deep desire to learn and share more about my history and culture.

As I highlighted in Note B, rap came from the Imbongi, the Griots, and the Oral Historians of South Africa, but in America, it took on a life of its own. Hip-hop became an expression of street culture, but it was still in step with the tradition of African life-force music. It became a lifeline for many low-income youths, and artists used rap as a form of social commentary. I had traveled the world many times over by this point and had encountered just about every type of music there was, but in 1979 hip-hop began to take over in a way that I had never seen before. When the group Sugar Hill Gang released "Rappers Delight," it sold about twelve million singles. When I visited places like Germany, Amsterdam, and Denmark, the kids knew every word of it.

The music industry at large, however, was pretty skeptical about whether or not rap would survive and remain a popular style. I was convinced, and had said so in many interviews, that rap was here to stay; we'd either have to keep up or be kicked out. I became increasingly vocal about it in the late 1980s, as demonstrated by my 1989 album *Back on the Block*. On it, I included contemporary rappers such as Ice-T, Melle Mel, Big Daddy Kane, and Kool Moe Dee. As previously mentioned in Note D#, it was written for a cross-cultural and cross-generational group of musicians. In addition to rappers, the album had the likes of Ella Fitzgerald, Luther Vandross, and Ray Charles. Beyond an attempt to create great music, there was a deeper meaning behind it.

I believed that the kids coming up needed to be introduced to jazz; most important, they needed to understand that all of our music and culture springs from the same roots. And I knew that hip-hop was the way to do it. There was such a disconnect between the various forms of expression, but I wanted to build a bridge. I had rappers Kool Moe Dee and Big Daddy Kane introduce their generation of hip-hoppers to Dizzy Gillespie, Miles Davis, and the jazz generation on a version of Joe Zawinul's classic *Birdland*.

Serendipitously, around the same time, my dear friend Steve Ross, the genius executive behind the Time Warner merger, asked me if I had any ideas for a project we could work on together. I had been dreaming of forming a coalition of the hip-hop nation to consolidate the music's energy in a meaningful way. So, in an effort to highlight the culture, instead of glorifying the theatrics of gangsta rap where people either get in trouble or killed, I shared my idea of creating a magazine that would give a more positive voice to the Black population. Shortly thereafter, in partnership with Steve and Time Warner, we created *Vibe* magazine in 1992.

We had Snoop Dogg on the cover of our very first issue, and in the world of music press, *Vibe* quickly became for hip-hop music what *Rolling Stone* magazine was for rock music. Even though critics placed a limit on how far we could go, I felt that the possibilities were endless, as it became one of the bestselling hip-hop magazine in the country at the time.

In the midst of celebrating the success of the magazine though, the backdrop of the "gangsta rap" scene was becoming increasingly dangerous in the mid-'90s, as lives were being lost. There were real bullets being exchanged during the height of the East Coast–West Coast hip-hop rivalry, and with the media controlling the narrative, a rapper murdered in plain sight was treated like a disposable asset to the hip-hop scene. Outlets continuously glorified these acts and made enemies out of the artists; stories being published were centered around the threat of rap, but failed to acknowledge the deeper issues of racism and why kids in the arena felt they had to go down a path of violence in the first place. When hip-hop made money, it was praised, but when someone got hurt, the public turned a blind eye to addressing the real issues. We couldn't afford to have that type of attitude. Not when real lives were at stake.

As further proof, in the April 1994 issue of *Vibe*, twenty-three-year-old rapper Tupac asserted from jail that "if we really are saying rap is an art form, then we got to be more responsible for our lyrics. If you see everybody dying because of what you saying, it don't matter that you didn't make them die, it just matters that you didn't save them. . . . Nobody ever came to save me. They just watch what happens to you. That's why Thug Life to me is dead. If it's real, then let somebody else represent it, because I'm tired of it. I represented it too much. I *was* Thug Life."

I wanted to help break down the feud between rap artists and the East and West Coast groups by talking to them about hope. After all, I was once headed down that path. I knew what it was like to think that joining a gang or turning to violence was my only escape, but because I had been liberated from that lifestyle, I couldn't leave them there alone. As a result, on August 24,

1995, at the Peninsula Hotel in New York City I organized a *Vibe* summit to address the state of hip-hop. I had Clarence Avant, Attallah Shabazz, Maya Angelou, General Colin Powell, and other thought leaders speak to the likes of Chuck D, P. Diddy, Common, Dr. Dre, Fab Five Freddy, Suge Knight, Q-Tip, Biggie, and more about how they couldn't let the struggles of the streets make them turn on each other, and to take responsibility for the type of music they put out. My other goal was to get the rappers to speak to each other, face to face, with some sense, and without the media in the way to fuel the fire.

During the symposium, American music executive (and my best friend) Clarence Avant said that "Talent is power.... You have to use it in a fashion where it benefits you, rather than destroys you." And Attallah Shabazz, Malcolm X's daughter, imparted that "we have to get into the habit of really liking ourselves—simply—in order to determine that when we do acquire the power, we have some sense of responsibility. [Do not be] retaliatory, [or] just motivated out of being pissed, or angry, or mad. [Because] that means somebody knows what button to push. If you just function pissed, I could always piss you off." Jake Robles of Death Row Records also said during one of the workshops that he'd "never seen a record make a person kill. [He'd] seen poverty make a person kill. [He'd] seen dope make a person kill. [He'd] seen the lack of dope make a person kill and try to go get it." Jake was shot and killed one month after the summit.

The media glorified rivalry, but when kids got wrapped up in it, they were left alone to deal with the responsibility.

I know that the symposium wasn't a complete fix all, but it started a much-needed dialogue within the hip-hop community and provided a bit of hope and perspective in the middle of an extremely dark time. The messages we shared at the summit clicked for some artists, and over time, I was made aware of how it positively impacted their careers—most important, their lives. I wanted to teach them that although fame, money, and violence may grant a faux sense of temporary power, it never lasts.

One and two years later respectively, Tupac and Biggie were taken far too soon. It absolutely burned me up, especially after having known these kids personally.

I will never, ever forget all of the lost souls.

In the following years, there were a lot of shifts in the senior leadership at *Vibe* and the collective vision began to splinter. Even though the dream didn't last, I don't look at it as a failure because it allowed me to connect with the pulse of the streets during a time in which no one else was.

In 2018, *Billboard* published an article that stated, "*Vibe* magazine was the first true home of the culture we inhabit today. Before top radio stations across the country branded themselves as places for 'hip-hop and R&B,' before TV shows and films and commercials regularly reflected hip-hop sensibilities, before mainstream publications regularly put people of color on their covers, *Vibe* launched with a confidence that all of these things would soon produce a new, multicultural mainstream."

Because I was able to step into the hip-hop world, a place that very few wanted to go, I had the opportunity to present a more positive narrative about our culture than the one that had previously been commercialized. It also provided me with a direct line of communication to cats who may have never had the chance to hear from someone like me—someone who came up in the same environment they did, and who could relate to their pain and struggles. I was able to share my personal experience about why gangs and violence were not the way to go. A lot of those kids had never had role models in their lives, and since they saw the media glorifying the downfalls of the gangsta rap environment, they gravitated toward it because it was the only dream they were taught to have.

Although the magazine's final outcome was not exactly as I had envisioned, I knew that if I had stopped myself from pursuing that dream, there never would have even been a *Vibe*. It opened doors for people of color to be shown on the front covers of a magazine, for kids to see a more holistic view of hip-hop that mainstream media didn't want them to see. Most important, it allowed for a dialogue centered around hope to take place.

Dreaming big has led me to heights that I never expected, and I've surprised myself with my ability to be stretched in so many different directions. I sure didn't know where my aspirations would take me, but in a way, I'm glad I didn't. If I had known, I may not have ever applied myself to the fullest extent, as a result of seeing how daunting the tasks ahead were. It's important to not give up on yourself before you've even tried, so keep dreaming and putting in the work to back up those dreams. Don't expect them to get accomplished on their own.

I have to warn you though: Big dreams don't come without big failures. Things will get tough and you will make mistakes.

Repeatedly. We're human and we're going to flounder, but it's what you do to get back up that matters. If I allowed myself to stay in the downward swings, then I'd still be there. Similarly, if you miss the mark on your first try, don't give up. Success is a cumulative process; it's not a one-time event. When you're just starting out, it's one mess-up after another. Winning one, then losing the next. After a little while, the "mess-ups" turn into valuable experiences. The more opportunities you have to win, lose, or barely make, the more chances you'll have to convert those experiences into fuel. You don't learn as much just from winning or playing it safe.

When I was coming up in the entertainment industry, I could never start a project with a lackadaisical attitude, even if it was a project that I didn't dig too much. I knew that they were all important, because if I did a bad job once, when it came to the next bebopper Hollywood would say, "Well, Quincy didn't do a good job, so no more soul brothers for us." I could never take that attitude. And now, when Black kids see me nominated for an Academy Award, they know it can be done.

You may not be able to do everything on your own, but by being the spark that ignites the flame, you just might be the impetus for change that you never thought was possible, helping to prevent the "firsts" from being the "onlys."

Imagine if everyone and their momma were waiting for someone else to take the lead, or to be the "first." I think the world would be an incredibly stagnant place. Whether creating a new piece of music, or building a new tech platform, or trying to cure cancer, or any number of other roles that you never thought you'd fill, we all have a position. Even when it comes to your art, taking risks and having the drive to create what has never been created before will undoubtedly set you apart from your peers. If you're not seeing the type of representation that you feel is necessary in your line of work, then take it upon yourself to change it. Don't limit yourself. Whether that's in the area of pursuing equality, creative freedom, or whatever else that looks like for you, step into the roles that aren't being filled. Oftentimes, our greatest creative challenges come from a place of inner change because we're pushed, pulled, and stretched into shapes, corners, and directions we never thought we'd occupy.

It's important to set lofty dreams in order to avoid outgrowing them because an ego is really just an overdressed insecurity. If I maintained small dreams as a kid, then I may not have seen any value in pushing myself toward more. If I had that attitude, then *Vibe* wouldn't have happened at the age of sixty.

I only hope to inspire those who come after me to make it happen—"it" meaning anything. May our collective efforts create many "firsts," but not "onlys."

UNDERSTAND

THE VALUE

OF

RELATIONSHIPS

F#

At this point in the scale, my hope is that you've internalized the lessons I've shared and will truly take them to heart. However, I must lead this Note with a warning: If you do everything correctly, but don't take heed to this next lesson I'm about to share, then it will all go to waste. So, please hear me when I say that you need to work on yourself just as much as you work on your art. As my former music teacher Nadia Boulanger always used to tell me, "Quincy, your music can never be more or less than you are as a human being." It doesn't matter how talented you are—or how many number-one hits you get—if you don't work on who you are, first.

If you're not a pleasant person to be around, believe me, word travels fast. I've seen way too many talented cats in this industry ruin their careers (and lives) as a result of failing to recognize this. And to set the record straight, your personal and professional endeavors are inextricably linked. What you do in your personal life affects how you are perceived in your professional life, and what you do in your professional life affects how you live your personal life. It's an important distinction to make, because what you do off the clock matters just as much as, if not more than, what you do in the office or studio.

You must have humility with your creativity, and grace with your success. Feelings of invincibility may start to creep in when you reach certain levels of achievements, but money and fame don't make you better than anybody else. Basic principles of human decency go hand-in-hand with your creative training. That's a fact. Every time I go to an event or party, I'm usually the last to leave because I spend time in deep conversations with anyone and everyone. I've heard people say, "It's incredible that you spent so much time talking with that clerk," or server, or fill in the blank. Well, why wouldn't I? As a matter of fact, why wouldn't you? Even if their work isn't directly related to yours, they are still a person who should be treated with respect. There's beauty in all people, and there's value in relationships.

Everything in this business, and life, revolves around relationships—the people you meet, and most important, how you treat them. You've really only got one shot at a reputation, and how you handle the relationships you develop along the way fills a big portion of that equation. I'm blessed to have been surrounded by people who were not only invested in my career, but also in me as a person.

I really learned the value of needing to work on myself first and as a musician second from the great bandleader and pianist Count Basie. It was a rough lesson to learn, but looking back, it changed the course of my life and career.

Remember when I told you in Note A# that Seattle was like a music mecca? Well, I'd often play hooky from school to hang out backstage of the Palomar Theatre, the Eagles Auditorium, and the Washington Social and Educational Club to get a glimpse of the touring jazz musicians. One such artist I had the honor of meeting at the Palomar was one of my ultimate idols, Count Basie. I was only thirteen, and I guess I was obviously so desperate for music advice that he basically adopted me. He didn't see me as a kid begging for help, but as a youngster with potential, who just needed a bit of guidance.

Back in those days, Black entertainers were like close family: They supported and cared about one another simply because of an unspoken kinship. In my case, Basie took it a step further and assumed whatever role he saw lacking in my life—an older brother, a mentor, a manager, anything. He taught me how to survive in life and in business. As exciting as the music industry can be, no one ever stays on top. Because he had been through the gamut, he prepped me for a similar journey. "Learn to deal with the valleys, because the hills will take care of themselves," he said. The hills are a metaphor for success. The valleys are a metaphor for when you have to pay your dues and get your butt kicked. That's the place you really learn about what you're made of, but you have to start there in order to get to the mountaintop. He made sure that I knew how to handle myself, whether I was at the top or the bottom, because success is never guaranteed.

In the early '60s, when I was struggling to get started with my own big band, he always offered support. He once signed a loan for me to get a $5,500 advance from a bank, even though there was no telling when I'd be able to pay him back. Through it all, he made sure everything was a learning experience, not a handout.

One of the hardest lessons to learn was to "always be fair." He got me and my band of eighteen musicians a gig in Hartford, Connecticut, subbing for his band, playing for the Black Shriners. The promoter was expecting eighteen hundred ticket buyers but only seven hundred people showed up. After the gig, I collected the money that was due to me, and was about to split town when Basie showed up unannounced and said, "Give the man half of his money back. He put your name out front, and people didn't show up. That's not his fault."

"Are you serious?" I asked.

Basie replied, "Your name was on the poster. You didn't draw. That ain't his fault. You may have to meet this promoter down the road again. Give him half the money back."

I did, but I was mad. I needed that money. I earned that money. Basie's lesson was to "always be fair," but it didn't feel fair. It was my money, plain and simple. And here came Basie to tell me what I couldn't do with it. Man, you bet I was mad, but I wouldn't dare talk back. I respected him too much.

In hindsight, I realize what he did. Through that one encounter, he taught me the importance of becoming a man of integrity because only then could I be a good businessman and musician. I could have walked away with the money since it was contractually mine, but because my name didn't deliver what it was expected to, acting in the best interest of the promoter was the right thing to do. Basie made sure that I treated people fairly, even if it meant getting the short end of the stick.

I don't think I ever saw that promoter again. But that's just it: Don't do things as a way to get something in return. Do it because it *is* the right thing to do. It might not feel like you get anything out of it, but that's exactly the point. It's not for you. It's the right thing to do. If you need further proof as to why you should live this way, I'm going to break it down a bit further. Beyond doing the right thing for the sake of doing the right thing, it leads to more meaningful relationships and saves you a lot of headaches in the long run.

When I was trying to assemble a big band for the *Free and Easy* tour that I mentioned in Note C, I knew that Basie had some of the best players in his band, and I could've easily poached some of them. But I didn't dare. Basie had been too good to me, and I wasn't about to stab him in the back. Preserving a person's trust is one of the most valuable things you can do, and when you make good relationships, you keep them for life.

Even though it was never my intention to try and get more out of people by keeping them around long enough, continued work opportunities were naturally afforded to me because I maintained my relationships. For example, when Frank Sinatra asked me to conduct him and the Count Basie Band for an album in 1964, it was like hitting the jackpot. As I mentioned in Note C#, the reason Frank asked me to conduct and arrange his record was that he heard the arrangement I did with Basie a year before. Do you think I would have been able to do that record with Basie if I had stayed mad at him after he made me return half of my money to that promoter in Hartford? I don't think so. Working with Frank and Splank (Basie's nickname) turned out to be one of the most special projects I have ever worked on. And aside from obvious perks of collaborating with musicians who turned into family, we wound up making history together with "Fly Me to the Moon" when it became the first song to be played on the moon. I got to share that special moment with my mentor, the cat who brought me up when he could've easily pushed me down many times.

It was also with Basie that I had the pleasure of working with the legendary Ella Fitzgerald. We did a record together called *Ella and Basie!* for the famed producer Norman Granz. After that project, I wound up working with Ella many more times. I can't even begin to tell you how many more examples I have of how meaningful personal relationships led to meaningful work relationships. The list goes on, and it hasn't failed me, personally or professionally.

Beyond the basic importance of building relationships, having the ability to establish a strong personal connection allows for a deeper sense of loyalty and camaraderie within your creative collaborations. For example, I've been using the same musicians for years because, aside from being monster musicians, they are genuine people. You feel it in the music. I get to know my players because if I don't know who they are as people, then I certainly won't know who they are as musicians. When I was working on Michael Jackson's records, I got the best of the best people in the room based upon real relationships. As previously mentioned, Rod "Worms" Temperton was one of the greatest songwriters, but he was also one of the greatest people I knew. It made the whole experience much more enjoyable, and besides, it's impossible to sit and listen to more than eight hundred songs with someone you don't get along with! He didn't have a drop of bs in his body. We kept everything super real with each other, and we exchanged strong opinions and comments without ever "throwing a wobbly," which was his British slang for "losing it." I've always been blessed to work with some of the best in the business, and I'm even more blessed to have gained them as members of my musical family. When you work with people whom you respect, you naturally get connected to their network of relationships, and it continues to build from there.

In 1984, when *Thriller* took the world by storm, I went to see Basie when he was playing a gig at the Palladium in Los Angeles. Little did I know that it would be the last time I'd ever see him. He was approaching eighty and in a wheelchair. And after the concert, he was wheeled over to me backstage. With eyes wide, he reached up, grabbed my arm and exclaimed, "Man—that shit you and Michael did, me and Duke would never even dream about nothin' that big. You hear me? We wouldn't even dare to *dream* about it!"

Basie had been there for me since I was thirteen. Looking down at him in that wheelchair was like looking down the long path of our thirty-seven-year relationship, which started with me staring up at him in the spotlights of the Palomar Theatre in Seattle. To get a compliment from him meant more than anything—more than fame or fortune. Awards and accolades come and go; money is spent, earned, and spent again: but there will never, ever be another Count Basie.

As a product of moving forward in life, you naturally leave a lot behind, but Basie reminded me of everything I had come from: my dad, my jazz roots, my past, my integrity. A few of my early jazz friends backed away from me as I gained more recognition. I wanted our relationships to be like they were before— fun, free, without strain or pretension—yet some still fell apart. Nothing small should ever be allowed to destroy a lifelong friendship, and Basie knew that. His love was unconditional. He was always proud of me, regardless of my accomplishments or what style of music I wanted to play. He was there for me, and vice versa. He was a king. When I looked down at him, sitting in that wheelchair, I knew he was dying. I could see it in his eyes. I said, "Thank you, Splank," and I hugged him and turned away, escaping to the dressing room before he could see my tears.

The lessons Basie shared are ingrained in me to this very day, and I always think of him when faced with either taking the easy way out or making the more difficult (and right) decision. I'm eternally grateful for the man he was in my life, and I don't think I'd be the same person without him.

It's funny, my best friend, the Black Godfather, Clarence "Bumps" Avant, used to joke that if I had twenty-seven cents, I'd give away twenty-five. He once wrote that he "never met anyone who could walk into a room and have grown men—seasoned, grizzled businessmen—hugging each other."

I'm aware that my actions may appear to be a bit "soft" at times, but I wouldn't trade my desire to be a decent human being for all the money in the world. I don't say this to fluff my own feathers, but to remind you that it's possible to find success while sticking to your morals. I know it's tempting to ignore them when you feel as though you're alone in the pursuit. Believe me, I know that doing the right thing isn't always publicly celebrated, but what you do when no one is watching is the foundation that you build your life and career on. Build it on solid ground and you'll be around until the end of time. But build it on sand, and you'll sink before the clock strikes twelve.

Sure, I may have lost out on money or opportunities here and there because I chose to take the high road, but it saved me a lot of headaches. Whether you believe in God, or karma, or the law of attraction, or don't believe in any of it, the common denominator of all of it is that when you act on principles, you attract those who carry themselves in a similar manner. When you treat people poorly, they will do the same with you. Of course, there are exceptions to this rule, but the majority of the time, it holds true. Knowing this truth has prevented me from winding up in bad business deals with people who didn't have my best interest at heart. Acting with integrity sets you apart from the crowd. It's easy to go with the flow and do things the way others do; it's much harder to go against the grain and act with a moral compass.

Beyond the ethical component of this lesson, many of the most successful people I've met throughout my lifetime are those who have mastered the concept of relationships and true connection. And, most important, they come to know an individual for who they are, not for what they do. One of the most memorable lessons I learned from the ultimate visionary, and my unconditional friend Steve Ross (former CEO of Time Warner), was to "be a bear, be a bull, but never a pig." You can't treat people like they're disposable because . . . they aren't.

In fact, I still work with most of the musicians that I assembled for my "Killer Q Posse" back in the '80s to this very day. There's more to people than what they can do for me in a business setting. And you know what? That's one of our biggest problems as a society. We reduce individuals to a number and a position. When you meet someone at a networking event, what's the first question you normally ask them? "So, what do you do for work?"

How many of your business partners or creative collaborators do you actually know? Do they have kids? Do they have hobbies? If you don't know the answers, then it's time to do some personal work. I usually ask my partners all kinds of questions about who they are as a human first, because I'm genuinely interested. Some of my favorites to ask are "What are your roots?" or "Where were you born?" Without emotional context, you're just there to make a transaction.

As you may have noticed by now, I've got nicknames for most of the people I work with. Without even trying, it establishes an automatic, personal relationship and breaks down any pre-existing barriers that professional associations tend to come with. It has become so natural to how I interact with people that I often forget about it until someone points it out. Find unique ways to connect with people, and you will discover even more enriching ways to relate. I've been asked, "How do you have so many friends?" Well, simply put, I try not to be a bad one.

Personally, I make a conscious decision to only work with collaborators I know to be genuine and trustworthy individuals. In fact, during all of the years I had the honor of working with Frank Sinatra and Ray Charles, we never once had a contract: only our word and a handshake. It was the most beautiful thing to know that we could trust each other, wholeheartedly. My word was my word, and it was the same for them. We never broke promises we made to each other or had public confrontations, and that's because we valued and respected each other. I know that working in a contract-free relationship may not be possible for everyone, but it's the underlying principle that matters. Mean what you say and say what you mean. I know the difference between working with those who have clearly taken the time to work on themselves, and those who haven't. The same goes for the people I hire at my company, Quincy Jones Productions. We operate like a family. It doesn't mean it's always sunshine, lollipops, and rainbows, but at the end of the day, I surround myself with good people I know I can rely on.

Without naming any names, I've come across plenty of individuals with whom I choose never to work again because they've shown me their true colors, on set or in the studio. You really only get one chance at a reputation, and I've seen plenty of people ruin relationships and opportunities before they've even had a chance to properly establish them. As you may find in your line of work, especially in the creative industry, it's a small world, and there are usually, at a maximum, only six degrees of separation. Whether you want to believe it or not, people talk, and they'll talk about you, too, for better or for worse. Hopefully this lesson will save you from ruining relationships because of your actions, or establishing a reputation that you can't recover from.

With the severity of cancel culture nowadays, this is nothing to play around with.

Although social media has many positive uses, the downside is that, with so much interaction taking place online, we've really lost a sense of personal connection. It's easy to hide behind a screen and act out of character because it doesn't seem like there will be consequences. But whether you see it or not, actions do have consequences. Maybe not now, maybe not tomorrow, but eventually. No matter how far we are pulled in the direction of interpersonal disconnection, never lose sight of who you are at heart, and never lose sight of humanity.

Acting without integrity might get you to a certain point, but the consequences of your actions will always catch up to you. All you have to do is read or watch the news to see such scenarios played out, as a result of poor, personal decision-making by once-revered individuals. *You* have to live with the consequences of your own actions, and I promise that the people who were once cheering you on to make bad decisions will no longer be around when you need someone to help pick you up.

My hope is that you will put in the necessary work to build a career that is established on the grounds of authenticity and credibility, rather than trying to conform to what is popular at any given moment. As I said before, you never have to make a comeback if you never leave, and building a career on firm morals will allow you to do so. It's a marathon, not a race. Don't treat others well just because you want something out of them. Treat people well because it's the right thing to do. Always work on yourself first because then, and only then, can you become a better musician, creative, executive, or whatever else it is that you strive to be. Make decisions that you can be proud of. If it leads to a positive opportunity for you, then great. If not, then at least you have a clear conscience. I'm tellin' you, gaining success is always more rewarding when you know you've achieved it as a result of genuine hard work, and not by cheating or getting there unethically.

So, once again, I'll leave you with what Nadia Boulanger taught me: "Your music can never be more or less than you are as a human being."

SHARE
WHAT YOU
KNOW

NOTE

G

One particular individual who exemplified what it meant to be
an exceptional musician, and an even better human being, was
the legendary trumpeter Clark Terry. Clark, or Sac, as we used
to call each other (short for sack-a-doo-doo! That's our bebop
sense of humor for ya \(ˆoˆ)/) was hands down one of the best
trumpet players, and his passion for mentorship was one of his
greatest gifts to this planet. He changed my life, Miles Davis's
life, Herbie Hancock's life, and the lives of everyone else he
chose to invest in. His belief in me as a kid greatly impacted the
course of my career, and as my very first trumpet teacher, his
encouragement has fueled me ever since, even after his passing

in 2015. His entire ninety-five years of life exemplified one of the most special lessons I've ever learned: the importance of mentorship, as both a mentor and mentee, a symbiotic relationship that has the power to transform lives.

I'll tell you more about *how* Sac managed to teach me this, but first I want to focus on *why* this type of relationship is so important.

Regardless of your desired field, your first few steps tend to be the most daunting because you have to face a steep learning curve, and establish yourself as a figure of authority, without having any prior experience. In my case, having started out with no prior music knowledge, it was essential to learn from those who had walked the road before me, so that I could take in as much knowledge from them as possible, and learn what *not* to do. The entertainment industry often portrays success as an overnight feat, but what isn't always depicted is the accumulation of mistakes needed to get to that place. So, when you look at someone and think, "He's got tremendous experience," or "She's super successful," that just means they've already made a lot of mistakes to get where they are, and you need the opportunity to do the same. You also need people around you who can say, "Don't do that, we already blew that twenty years ago," to save you from the potentially career-ending or life-threatening hiccups. *Those* are your mentors.

In addition to other benefits, mentorship has set me on a fast track to my goals. Instead of wasting time searching far and wide for answers, I've been able to glean advice from those who had already been through the wringer. Even if they didn't have all of the solutions, their guidance served as an advanced start-ing point. And since you will undoubtedly be faced with tough decisions and put in difficult situations, a mentor can help you navigate the waters that they've already passed through.

Without the musical and personal giants who put me on their shoulders and helped me see that I could achieve more than I ever thought possible, I don't believe I would be here now. The accumulation of external guidance instilled a sense of belief within me when, at times, I had none in myself. And most important, my mentors have been essential guideposts, putting me back on track whenever I veered off course.

Conversely, *being* a mentor is just as important as having one; if somebody puts you on their shoulders, it should be your responsibility to do the same for someone else. If God gives you talent in any area of your life, it's up to you to be a good steward of that gift and pass it along. Stewardship helps create a stronger bond between generations, while also instilling in individuals a sense of belief that has the power to transform entire popula-tions. There really would be no such thing as a generation gap, if we only had enough people willing to lift each other up, instead of tear each other down. To echo the sentiment of the age-old adage, "The youth are our future," and we need to invest in them.

Mentoring is often assumed to require a formal structure, but I promise that you don't need to have any special skills to have a mentor, or to be one. A mentor is simply *anyone* who can see the question marks or glimmer of hope in your eyes. There is no rulebook for how to be a mentor, other than the fact that you just have to stay true to a desire to make a difference in someone else's life. There's no secret to it. Oftentimes, all a person needs is a sense of belief, and in my case, Clark Terry's confidence in me went a long way. As beloved jazz bassist Christian McBride notes, Clark "taught thousands of students who have taught thousands of students, who are going to teach thousands of students." One simple act has the power to go a long way, so don't underestimate the impact that you can have on those you come into contact with.

Well, now that I've shared *why* I believe in the power of mentoring, stick with me for one of my favorite stories: the story behind *how* Clark became my mentor.

As referenced in the last Note, when I was a kid, I'd frequently hang around backstage at local theaters in Seattle (yes, that was allowed back then) just so that I could catch a glimpse of what the touring musicians were up to. From their slang to their playing, I was set on absorbing every bit of it. Since this was 1947, before TV had really taken off, hanging out at the hot spots was really my only chance to find out about the latest musical licks from the East Coast. So, when the Count Basie Band was at the Palomar Theatre for a month-long residency that year, I was hell-bent on being there every single night. Clark was a trumpeter in Basie's band, and as a result of radio communication, everybody in town knew that Clark was *the* trumpet player of all trumpet players. Finding my way backstage was like being mere steps away from a musical god. I was just a scrawny thirteen-year-old, and all I wanted to do was see if he could give me some advice. Night after night I'd return to hear the band play, and watch as they departed, until one day I worked up enough courage to approach Clark and asked if he'd be willing to teach me how to play the trumpet properly.

After entertaining the idea for a minute, he quickly concluded that it wouldn't be possible because he'd have to play at the theater 'til late, then at clubs until the middle of the night, and then he wouldn't get back to his hotel until the early morning, and after that, he'd sleep during the day until he'd have to do it all over again.

After a second thought, he reconsidered. "Well, you're in school while I'm sleeping. And you're sleeping when I'm working. How are we gonna solve that?"

I knew it was a long shot, but I also knew it was my only chance, so I had to figure something out quickly.

"Well, I could get up early and come to you before I go to school for a couple of hours," I replied.

To my surprise, he agreed. The very next day at six A.M. I showed up at his hotel room soon after he had fallen asleep, and knocked on the door to wake him up.

I returned every day that month, and he taught me everything from technique to style to diaphragmatic breathing. My mouth used to bleed when I played because I held my trumpet incorrectly, so he caught it and said, "No, turkey, put it up here," as he signaled higher up on his lip. The lessons he taught me were endless, and during the last week, when Clark was getting ready to cut out of town with Basie for their next gig, I came over to his hotel and said, "Mr. Terry, I've learned to write too, and I would appreciate it if you'd listen to my first arrangement here."

"I'm leaving, but give it to me and I'll look at it when we get to San Francisco."

When he got to San Francisco, he passed it around to Basie and asked if he "remembered that little kid in Seattle who used to hang around the bandstand." After Basie acknowledged that he did, in fact, remember me, he agreed to try it out. They played it, and apparently it was a little tired, but Clark believed in me so much that when he returned to Seattle for more dates, he returned my chart with some encouraging words: "Kid, you made a couple of mistakes, but I can tell you're really on the right track. You're gonna be a major talent someday."

"You really think so?"

"I know so," he replied.

The belief he had in me was what kickstarted the confidence to keep working on my composition. As I mentioned in Note B, that was the composition I called "From the Four Winds" that eventually landed me a coveted spot in Hamp's band and a ticket out of Seattle.

In 1959, twelve years after my early-morning trumpet lessons with Clark, he and trombonist Quentin Jackson departed Duke Ellington's band to join mine on the *Free and Easy* tour. I couldn't believe it. It truly was one of the biggest honors of my life and all I wanted to do was make Clark proud.

Even after witnessing what a failure of an endeavor that tour turned out to be, he stuck with me through it all and then some. He was not only a mentor, a teacher, and a fellow musician; he was also a friend, a father, and a lifelong source of inspiration.

I often think back to that day in Seattle when I built up the courage to approach Clark and ask him for lessons; I will always be grateful for his altruistic act of teaching me in the early mornings, when he could have been sleeping. He believed in my potential, and he was considerate enough to encourage me. His unfailing support supplied me with hope that I could some-day be like him. And it didn't end with me. Clark's impact was far-reaching, as he went on to mentor generation after genera-tion of jazz musicians. Through it all, he never charged a student for a lesson.

In 2014, I co-produced a documentary called *Keep On Keepin' On*, which highlights Clark's beginnings as a trum-peter and pioneer in early American jazz, and his mentorship of Justin Kauflin, a killer pianist, composer, educator, and record producer. It's an incredible story in and of itself, but the back-story of how the film came to be is altogether inspiring.

Clark and I remained close after the years he taught me, playing together on albums and in concerts, and his impact remained very tangible in my life. But by the early 2000s I had come to the unfortunate conclusion that some of the younger generation did not properly recognize the incredible contri-butions that Clark and his contemporaries made to America's musical lexicon. I was sick and tired of the fact that students aren't always taught the value of jazz and blues history, and I wanted to do something about it. I then decided to pur-sue a record with Snoop Dogg rapping, and Clark doing his

"Mumbles" routine (a sort of scat singing that eventually became his signature sound). I thought it would be the perfect bridge between the older and younger generations. Hip-hop, after all, emanated from bebop.

After more than a year of planning for the recording, I arrived at the airport in Little Rock, Arkansas, with Adam Fell, the president of my company, only to receive a call confirming that Snoop had unfortunately sprained his ankle and wasn't going to make it. We were prepared to scrap the entire plan, but instead of hopping back on the plane, we continued to make the drive to Pine Bluff to see Clark and his wife, Gwen. Without Snoop, we had no pressing work to finish anymore; so, what would have been a hectic day trying to produce a record, turned into a "hang-thang." At the house, Clark introduced me to his new student, Justin Kauflin (and Justin's best guide dog, Candy), and asked Justin to play the piano for me. This kid was a monster on the keys, and he played with such authority and mastery, despite the fact that he had been blind since age eleven.

Clark also introduced me to a few others at the house: two guys from Australia—Alan Hicks (director) and Adam Hart (cinematographer)—and their wonderful producer Paula DuPré Pesmen who were collectively making a documentary about Clark.

They showed me a working trailer for their film that night, which prompted me to get involved as a co-producer from that point forward.

The director of the documentary, Alan Hicks, shares the following:

I wasn't the best student in high school. In fact, I was probably one of the worst students in school. I picked up drumming after seeing a young kid play, and one day a teacher said he was putting together a jazz band. I practiced all the time and it changed me, it became like a discipline. After that I was hooked. When I was eighteen, I moved from Australia to Brooklyn, New York, in 2002. I wanted to be in the place where it was all happening—where every jazz musician was aspiring to go. On the plane ride over, I read *Q: The Autobiography of Quincy Jones*, which included a chapter written by Clark Terry. I didn't have much of a plan when I came to New York. I applied to a bunch of schools and got accepted to study music at William Paterson University. I was having an incredible experience, but after a year I was dead-broke, so I booked a ticket back to Australia. My teacher at the time was the late great piano player James Williams. When I told James I was going home, he invited me to a concert at the Blue Note Jazz Club to see the Oscar Peterson Trio. He knew I wouldn't miss a chance to see those guys play. I walked in and he sat me down at a table next to Clark Terry and his wife, Gwen. I was floored to be sitting next to a living legend. Clark turned to me and said, "You must be Al. James told me about you and he says you can play. I think it's a bad idea for you to move home. You should stick with your studies here, man." Before I could think, he invited me to

153

dinner at his house one week later. He knew it was after my departure date. There was no way I could miss this once-in-a-lifetime opportunity, so I changed my flight. After dinner that night, he said to me, "Come for dinner next week, and bring your sticks." Following that night, I spent thousands of hours playing in Clark's bands and touring the world with him. Even if I'd only met him that one night at the Blue Note, I would have cherished it for the rest of my life. I'm sure that Justin, the student featured in the film opposite Clark, feels the same way. Making this film was the first time I had ever been in charge of anything. What I know about being a leader, I learned from Clark. He taught me how to put together a band and how important it is to surround myself with good people. He told me, "The better they are, the better *you* sound." He also taught me to follow my gut instinct, push people gently in the direction of their best work, and lead by example. I tried to bring all of this to the film. When I started shooting, I didn't have much frame of reference. Because I had never made a film before, I mostly had to draw on what I had learned playing music—what I learned from Clark. I discovered there were various parallels between filmmaking and jazz. There's a lot of intuition in both. Jazz is improvisation with a form. Structure is important; a song needs a beginning, middle, and an end. Sometimes when I was editing, I would approach a scene like that. I'd have to hear it in my head, like a song. That's how I see the whole film. Clark once told me that when you feel your nerves start to creep up and everything inside of you is telling you not to get up there and play, that's when you should play because that's when you're going to learn something about yourself. He said, "Embrace the nerves." This is what I've tried to do with the film.

Keep On Keepin' On went on to win more than fourteen awards, including Best Documentary Feature at the Tribeca Film Festival. But most important, it served as a springboard for Clark's story and passion for mentorship to touch even more lives. In partnership with educational institutions, we've conducted hundreds of educational screenings of the film, and have shared supplementary educational resources for students to dissect, as a way to teach them about the history of jazz and blues and the importance of mentorship. Our hope is that students far and wide will be able to internalize the inspiration that Clark shared with me, Justin, Alan, and every other student who had the honor of studying under his guidance.

As further evidenced in the documentary, mentorship is not always one-sided. If anything, it's apparent that Justin taught Clark just as much as Clark taught Justin. Over the course of filming, Clark lost his sight due to diabetes, and had a really difficult time adjusting. But Justin's ability to share his experience about having lost his sight seven years earlier, due to exudative retinopathy, really helped provide Clark with a new perspective. Justin communicated how music served as an overall form of expression while also helping him to cope with his sudden inability to do things he used to be able to do.

Simultaneously, Clark, Justin, and I all have synesthesia, which is a neurological condition in which the stimulation of one sensory or cognitive pathway leads to an automatic trigger of another sensory or cognitive pathway. For instance, when we hear music, we see corresponding colors. With our mutual bond over Clark, synesthesia, and simply great music, I signed Justin to my management roster at Quincy Jones Productions, which completed one full circle of a story. It has been said that "coincidence is God's way of remaining anonymous," and I couldn't think of a more fitting summary of this whole encounter.

There truly aren't enough words to describe the depth of Clark's impact on music and humanity, but I will do my best. He was one of the first Black staff musicians for NBC's *The Tonight Show*, where he played for twelve years; and above all, he was a master mentor. Clark broke racial barriers and opened a whole lot of doors for musicians. He was born in 1920 to a dirt-poor family with eleven kids in St. Louis, Missouri. His mother passed away when he was seven years old. After hearing the Duke Ellington Band when he was ten years old, he fell in love with the sound of the trumpet. Since he couldn't afford one, he went to the junkyard where he constructed his own out of a kerosene funnel, a hose, and a lead pipe (which he later learned was poisonous!). Eventually his neighbors took notice of his interest in the trumpet and pooled together enough money to buy him a real one, which led him to jazz.

Can you imagine if his neighbors dissuaded him from playing the trumpet? Clark also once stated, in reference to our relationship, "You know, I can't help but think: What if I'd said, 'Kid, put that stuff up on a shelf, forget it, do something else.' What would've happened? I don't even like to think about it." I don't, either!

From the moment I asked him for trumpet lessons as a thirteen-year-old kid in 1947, to his very last breath in 2015, Clark made it a priority to invest in the younger generation. I was his first student and Justin was his last. Justin and I are fifty-three years apart, but Clark's belief in us at different stages of our lives influenced us both equally.

I hope that this Note, as well as the film, makes it abundantly clear that each and every one of you has a very special and unique gift to share with others. Clark didn't have time to teach me back in Seattle; he made the time. He would forgo sleep to give me lessons early in the morning, because he cared. He once stated, "You could tell that [Quincy] wanted to learn, he wanted to know. And because I was able to show him some things, that made me happy. That's what stirred my heart. I could help this kid." Those who come after us are the future, plain and simple. You don't need to be some type of celebrity or have a massive platform to be mentored or to become a mentor; it simply comes down to finding someone who believes in *you*, and finding someone else you believe *in*.

Think about a figure you respect, then learn everything about what they did and do. The main way to further understand how people before you have made it to where they are is to watch, pay attention, shut up, and listen. All I wanted was to hear what Clark had to say. It takes a lot of courage to go after a cat like that, but, as I often say, if you don't ask, you'll never get. You may receive a lot of "noes" but you also just might receive a "yes."

The knowledge my mentors passed down has lasted me a lifetime, so now, when kids come up to me after shows, it's a special feeling to keep that same line of communication open as best as I can. I may not know everything, but it makes my soul smile to share what I do know with those willing to listen. And honestly, I hope that I still won't have all of the answers when I'm one hundred, because learning is essential to growth, and I always want to continue growing.

I've been a passionate advocate for mentorship for many years. In fact, back in 2008, I teamed up with my brother Usher for a PSA about National Mentoring Month via the Harvard School of Public Health to share our perspective on how mentorship shaped our lives. I've been doing my best to share this message for many years, and I will continue to do so, because if it has the power to touch even a single person's life, then it's all worth it.

If you've been on this planet as long as I have, I hope we can all agree that it's incredibly important to be there for our young brothers and sisters. We can either beat them down, or build them up. For the record, I choose to build them *up*. I just might even be able to hitchhike a ride to the future with them! As the saying goes, "We go faster alone but further together."

I have tried my best to never disappoint those who have graciously placed their time and trust in my life and career. They helped keep me in the light when my world was filled with darkness. I'll never forget what it felt like to lose my mother to dementia praecox. I'll never forget being denied jobs based on the color of my skin. I'll never forget a lot of things that happened to me. But I will also never forget when the legendary Clark Terry accepted my request to teach me how to play the trumpet when he had absolutely nothing to gain from doing so. I will never forget when the great Nadia Boulanger took me under her wing to teach me the ins and outs of jazz, counterpoint, melody, and the foundation that I needed to become the musician I am today. I will never forget Count Basie's support and efforts to teach me how to be a man of integrity. I will never, ever forget. My mentors have undoubtedly shaped the person I am today, and without their love and guidance, I might still be stuck in the darkness of my past.

So, may we all continue to keep the light on for ourselves and for others. As Clark always used to quote from *The Three Stooges*, "If at first you don't succeed, keep on suckin' 'til you do suck a seed!"

RECOGNIZE

THE VALUE

OF LIFE

Now that we've reached the final Note in the scale, I must say that it's wonderful to achieve goals and reach a certain level of success, but when it's all said and done, what's the point? It's a question that I've been faced with many, many times, after having almost faced death many, many times. If you're not careful, stacking up material accomplishments and possessions may provide a temporary sense of fulfillment, but only at the juncture of life and death did I come to learn that the simple, yet complex, gift of living life itself is the ultimate achievement.

It's impossible to live as long as I have without getting very well acquainted with mortality. After all, I did attend my own funeral service. (We'll get there in a bit.) I thank God that my previous encounters with death didn't end with a finale, but being that close to it forced me to do some thinking—a lot of thinking, actually. It led me to the realization that, as a self-diagnosed workaholic, my family and health unfortunately took a back seat for more years than I'd like to admit. However, despite all the special awards and testimonials that maturity bestows, I've found that the values I carry within myself, and the impact I have on my family and beyond, carry the greatest weight.

There's nothing wrong with striving for more; I highly encourage it, but I'd also tell you to ask yourself why you are doing it. You may be surprised at your answer, but even more commonly, you may be surprised to not even have one. Careers are volatile and status comes and goes, but when it's all said and done, what legacy will you be proud to leave behind? And what will you be proud to have done with the time you've had? I'll tell you all about how I came to answer these questions for myself, but first I need to take you back with me to a few monumental moments in my life where my supposed endings became beginnings.

1947

As you may recall from Note C#, the first official band that I played in was fronted by the legendary bandleader Bumps Blackwell. Bumps was incredibly influential in the Seattle area and he was also commander in chief of the Army National Guard Band. You had to be eighteen to enlist, but since my bandmates and I were close with Bumps, he allowed us to stretch our ages on paper; we were only fourteen. This "gig" turned out to be a much bigger commitment than I'd expected, after I was sworn in as part of the all-Black Washington National Guard 41st Infantry Division Band. I went on active duty for two or three months during the summer in the Army at Camp Murray. My bandmates and I didn't even know how to do a "left face"! But, we sounded good and that's all that mattered—not to our sergeants, but definitely to us.

Toward the end of my tenure in the band, one of our assignments was to play a rodeo in Tacoma, so my four bandmates and I piled into a car and headed south. We were well on our way, laughing and practicing, but within a fraction of a second, everything changed. A Trailways bus came from out of nowhere and pummeled straight into our car.

I've spent a lot of time trying to block out the exact details of what happened that day, but what I can tell you is that many lives were lost. Three people on the bus were killed, and out of all the guys in my car—two up front, two in the back, and me in the middle—all of them died.

It didn't make any sense that I made it out alive. I tried to pull one of my friends out of the front seat, but he had been decapitated from the impact. It was, and still is, one of my most traumatic experiences. To this day, I have never learned how to drive.

1969

When the notable director Peter Yates asked me to score his movie *Bullitt*, I was gutted because I wasn't well enough to accept, due to a recent appendectomy. But later, when my dear friend and starring actor Steve McQueen asked me to come see the rough cut, I was happy to attend. I went with my hairdresser and good friend, Jay Sebring, who was also Steve's hairdresser. After leaving the screening, Jay invited me to Sharon Tate and Roman Polanski's home on Cielo Drive in Los Angeles for a get-together. Roman was still in London, but Sharon and a few other industry people were expected to be there.

As everyone does when they become a bit "wiser," I was starting to go bald in some spots. So, Jay had promised to give me some type of miracle hair-growth serum to help bring the shine down a bit and fill it back in with some hair. He told me: "I'll meet you at Sharon's tonight, because I've found something for your 'chintz' patch."

Jay and I made plans to meet up later in the evening and went our separate ways.

To be honest, I don't recall what consumed my attention for the rest of the night, but whatever it was, I simply felt too tired to go to the party and ended up falling asleep at home.

The following morning, my slumber was violently interrupted by what has remained one of the most earth-shattering phone calls I've ever received. From the other end of the line, my ears were met with seven words that are forever etched into my memory: "Did you hear about Jay? He's dead."

My knee-jerk reaction was to say, "B.S. I was just with him yesterday."

I hung up in disbelief and immediately called Jay's company, Sebring International. "Is Jay Sebring there?" I asked in a quavering voice.

The woman on the other side demanded, "Who is this?"

"Quincy Jones."

"Jay Sebring is dead," she firmly asserted before hanging up the phone.

I turned on the news and an immediate wave of horror enveloped me as I saw body bags strewn across the lawn of Sharon's house. The bags contained the precious bodies of every individual who had attended the party, including Jay. As news unraveled around what was later deemed the Manson Family/Tate Murders, I, along with the rest of the world, discovered what exactly took place at the Tate household—except I was supposed to be there. In the immediate aftermath, it was unclear as to who had committed the crimes, so security was on high alert throughout Los Angeles. People suspected each other, causing heightened tensions amongst civilians, until Sharon Tate's father, who was in military intelligence, led investigators to none other than Charles Manson. It turned out that Manson had ordered his "family," or rather, his cult followers, to target the previous owner of the home—the Beach Boys' famed producer, Terry Melcher—because he had denied Manson's request to do a record together.

I had known Sharon fairly well and had actually almost previously bought her house in the late '60s, but since the owner at the time was only open to renting, I decided to buy a house from actress Janet Leigh, on Deep Canyon Drive, instead. The tricks that this reality played on my mind were almost incomprehensible. I couldn't help but think: If I had moved into that house instead of Terry, it would have never been a target to begin with and everyone there might still be alive today. On top of that, what if I was there that night? It's a useless thought process, but there's still a part of me that keeps trying to make sense of such a senseless situation.

1974

By this time, I had been married and divorced twice. At age forty-one, I settled down with my girlfriend, Peggy Lipton, who later became my wife and the mother of two of my daughters, Kidada and Rashida. After working nonstop for three days and three nights on my album *Mellow Madness*, I was at home in Brentwood, California, when a terrible pain shot through my head. It felt as though someone had blown through the back of my brain with a shotgun. When I tried to sit up, the pain overtook me and I fell into a coma.

Peggy found me before it was too late, and rushed me to the hospital. I later found out that the main artery to my brain had burst. During a seven-and-a-half-hour operation, the doctors had to remove blocks of my skull like it was an igloo. I was given a 1-percent chance of survival. After the procedure, with my head fully wrapped in bandages, the doctors told me, "The good news is that you lived. The bad news is that you've got another one, and we've got to go back in." They had found another artery that was about to burst, so I had to go under the knife again.

The first aneurysm was an out-of-body experience during which I imagined God beckoning my spirit up to Him; but I wasn't about to go out, though. It was as if the doctors cleaned out all the cobwebs when they were up there. I contemplated everything I had yet to do: all of the grudges I had held, the people I needed to forgive, the people I needed to ask for forgiveness from, and the loose ends I needed to tie up. Most important, I thought about my rugrats—the kids that I had helped bring into this world. My daughter Kidada, only five months old at the time, still hadn't called me Daddy yet and I couldn't bear the thought of leaving this planet without ever having heard those words, or leaving her to face life without her father. I couldn't deny the fact that no matter how hard I tried to be a good father, I had still failed my children in some of the areas that they needed me most. Although I knew I was doing my best, my conscience knew that I had not been fully present in their lives; all I'd ever known was how to run in pursuit of "more."

After the bleak outcome of my first operation, a group of friends from the music industry prepared what was supposed to be a memorial for me at the Shrine Auditorium in Los Angeles. The operation was in August, and the memorial in September, but since I survived, it turned out to be a celebration-of-life concert. One of my doctors, Dr. Grode, and I sat up in a guest box, and it hit me that I was attending what was meant to be my own funeral. The show was conceived and produced by Peter Long, who I'd previously worked with on another production, as well as the always-supreme concert promoter Darlene Chan. It was a mind-boggling affair and they had just about everybody I could've imagined in the lineup: Cannonball Adderley with Freddie Hubbard in the band, Sarah Vaughan, Minnie Riperton, the Main Ingredient with Cuba Gooding Sr. on lead vocals, Ray Charles, Billy Eckstine, the Watts Prophets, and Marvin Gaye.

Roscoe Lee Browne did a recitation, as did Brock Peters, Sidney Poitier, and Richard Pryor. I couldn't get too excited though. My neurosurgeon, Dr. Milton Heifetz, previously told me that too much stimulation could be detrimental, as a result of the metal implants they'd placed in my brain, the same implants that stripped me of ever being able to play my trumpet again.

2015

Although I cleaned up my act in regard to how I treated and cared for my family (which had grown to seven children in total), I continued mistreating my body as a result of my poor eating and drinking habits. Everywhere I went, vodka or a drop of my 1961 Chateau Petrus would follow. It was my way of life, and that's all I had known for the previous sixty-plus years. Well, on January 7, 2015, I had pulled the last straw and slipped into a diabetic coma. I was once again rushed to the hospital in an ambulance, and lost four conscious days of my life. As I sat there in my hospital bed, that cliché that you always see happen in movies really happened to me: My life flashed before my eyes. The feeling was reminiscent of the one I had on my *last* death bed, following my aneurysms. It was all too familiar, but I was determined to make it past this one because I wasn't about to let my end be the result of my *own* actions. I didn't have a choice when it came to getting into a car accident, or having an aneurysm or an appendectomy, but I did have a choice when it came to partaking in activities that had no positive effect on my life. I'm talking about smoking cigarettes, drinking alcohol, you name it. I was determined to come correct if I came out of it, and man, I thank God I did. After that last wake-up call, I was forced to do a lot of reflecting.

We often think of life as a series of events that happen to us. As a result, we neglect the fact that it's often a series of actions that we do to ourselves. Having grown up under the guidance of jazz cats back in the '40s and '50s, I've seen and done the hard drug route, and I used to smoke four packs of cigarettes in a twenty-four-hour period. Coming up with the likes of Ray Charles and Frank Sinatra, I feel as though I've had enough alcohol for forty thousand people! I mean it. That lifestyle persisted and it probably still would today if it weren't for my most recent fling with death.

Oftentimes, what people don't realize is that everything, even physical health, starts in the mind. It's the most powerful thing you own. It can bring you to an evergreen pasture, but it can also take you down the darkest of roads. Putting all mental disorders aside, reaching that level of awareness is solely in your own hands. Without making a conscious effort to change your thought process, and subsequently your actions, nothing will change. It took a few wake-up calls for me to get there, but man am I grateful I finally made it. My hope for you is that you won't wait for your call; instead, I hope that you will simply take these stories of mine as a reminder to make any necessary changes.

The tricky thing about life is that you have to continuously reflect on your growth. A habit is a habit for a reason. They're hard to shake, and it's easy to forget lessons you've learned once they're in the rearview mirror. Personally, it has been astounding to look back on my life, because my memories have become so clear without the all-consuming presence of alcohol. I've been able to remember events from my past that I'm not sure I would have been able to otherwise, and now during important family moments, I am thankful to know that my recollection of them won't be clouded by my own poor drinking habits. After cleaning up my act in 2015, it felt like I could see clearly in every possible direction.

I say all of this not to put myself on a pedestal; rather, I'm just thankful for the fact that I am *still* here, and that's exactly why I set out to share all that I've shared in this book. Now, don't get me wrong, I still don't have it all figured out. I may be eighty-eight, but as I sit here writing this, I am even being reminded of some of the lessons I thought I had already learned. If a story made it onto these pages, odds are that it taught me something, and I hope it will do the same for you.

From a very young age, my only way "out" of the danger-ous places I was born into was through racking up accomplish-ments. At every stage of my life, those successes came at a greater expense than before; whether it was my family or my health, one was indirectly put on the chopping block. However, my life is more full now than ever because I can answer the question of *why* I do what I do: family, spreading hope and love through my creativity, and to hopefully have a positive impact in the lives of those I encounter.

If you don't know your answer yet, don't wait for a freak accident or a brush with death to start thinking about it.

Although experiencing a sense of loss may indirectly help you appreciate life in the long run, there's absolutely nothing like celebrating while you're still living it. After my fifth daughter Rashida and my brother-from-another-mother Alan Hicks (the same director I did *Keep On Keepin' On* with) released my latest documentary, *QUINCY*, on Netflix in 2018, I had even more to reflect on. This time, my life really flashed before my eyes, and I could see the entire arc of it: the struggles and the successes, as well as the nuances I could only notice when I took a look from the outside. There's absolutely nothing like seeing every pivotal moment of your life on the big screen and, on top of it, sharing those moments with the world. It is incredibly humbling and more than a reminder of everything I've been able to do; it is also a reminder of everything else I still want to do.

My first reaction after seeing the film was truly, "I wish I could live forever." It's obvious that I can't, but I wish I could. I read one review from a critic that said I come across as "insatiable" in the film, and I guess to some extent they're right. As humans, we're built with an insatiable appetite for wanting more; I mean, think about the fact that kids already know how to gesture or say the word "mine" when they want something, before having been taught. It's hard to deny the desire to always want more. I've been asked many times, "Don't you think you've done enough already?" I guess it might seem as though I have, but even still, there are things I still want to do. I still want to write a street opera. I still want to put out more records. Movies. Broadway plays. But beyond that, I want to see my babies, and my babies' babies, grow to see my age and beyond. I still want to do many, many things that I may or may not ever accomplish. It's a hard pill to swallow, but it's one that I must.

You may have started reading this book with hopes that I'd reveal some grand secret about how to get nominated for eighty Grammy® Awards, or how to achieve your highest creative self, but with age, I can assure you that simply being alive *and* present in your everyday life is the highest form of creativity.

After my aneurysms, the doctor told me that deep in our subconscious each of us has either a life force or a death wish. He said those who have a death wish can be taken out by something as common as the flu. But the ones who have a life force are usually the ones who survive. When the doctors operated on my brain, they had to tie my hands down because even under all the anesthesia the doctors used, my body was shaking. Or as I like to think of it, I was still fighting to survive.

When it's all said and done, I feel tremendously blessed to be here, especially for as long as I have been. I don't forget the moments when I was almost taken out because it makes the moments I have here that much more special. Life is an absolute trip and you never know what's going to come next. But, I'm telling you right now: Recycle your pain, if you can see it you can be it, go to know, establish your guideposts, always be prepared for a great opportunity, sharpen your left brain, avoid paralysis from analysis, understand the power of being underestimated, do what's never been done before, value relationships, and most important, recognize the beauty and inherent value of life. And tell your family—I'm not just talking about blood relatives—that you love them. Tell your friends you miss them. Be there for people, not only when they need you, but even when they don't.

At the end of the day, give life your full attention. When you step outside, take a moment to appreciate the seemingly unimportant details that you've neglected: from the feeling of receiving a nice warm hug from a friend whom you haven't seen in years, to the simplicity of being able to think and act on your thoughts. How incredibly astonishing. As minuscule as they may seem, not everyone has the same opportunities, and if you're sitting here reading this book right now, odds are you have some type of privilege that has even allowed you to read in the first place.

By transforming my mindset into one that's being present and grateful for every moment, I've found that the quality of my life *and* work has immensely improved. People keep asking me how I still have so much energy in my late eighties, and why I'm still actively engaged in the creative process, in both my own art and that of others. Well, my answer is, you can either choose to use what you've got, or lose what you've got, so I'm going to keep on usin' it. I'm incredibly thankful for this life that I live, and for the ability to think, work, and create. But it doesn't happen by accident. I had, and still have, to nurture my desire to grow as a human, regardless of whether or not it directly relates to my career. After all is said and done, as long as I'm alive and able to, I can and will keep creating. And as long as you're alive and able, you can and should keep creating. There is always more to experience, to make, and to share.

With that said, I can't help but remember the words of my beloved little brother, Lloyd. Before his unbearable passing in 1998, he told me that one of the things you realize when you're dying is that you've wasted a lot of time. When one particular individual, who didn't know that Lloyd was retiring due to a cancerous tumor in his kidney, asked Lloyd how he was going to identify himself after retirement, he responded with: "I can identify myself a hundred different ways. I'm a man. An engineer. A carpenter. A husband. A brother. A father. I'm a bicyclist. A skater. A skier. Shit. I'm a lot of things. But one thing I'm not, is a quitter."

His strength, even in the midst of an ultimate breaking point, was one of the most heart-wrenchingly beautiful reminders of how important it is to live the life that we've been given, while we still have it. I'm a blessed survivor of many close casualties, and that's a fact I try to honor and thank God for every day that I have breath to breathe.

But it's not just mental strength and a positive attitude that determines quality of life. If that alone was true, I'd be kickin' it for another eighty years, easily. In my line of work and industry, I frequently see young cats out there living their lives as if they are indestructible. I know how it feels to live this way, but I always want to sit them down and tell 'em to slow down a little. Stop drinking like there's no tomorrow. Stop stressing over the little things. Stop damaging your health. Your body will thank you when you're my age. Although my body isn't quite as resilient as it used to be, I still have to thank it for all of the miles it let me rack up. Respect the territory that you've been given to work on. Lord knows that hasn't always been easy for me.

It's strange to be close to hitting eighty-nine and feel like I'm thirty-five. Who knew what no alcohol and treating your body well could do? Let's take care of what we have while we have it, and spread love instead of hate, especially during times that test our humanity. We've all been put on this planet for a reason, and there's no use spending the minutes we have trying to create enemies. The only choice we have now is to either fight or unite, and please hear me when I say, the *only* answer is to *unite*!

Today, and every day, I'm overwhelmed by the love that I have for my rugrats—each and every one of them. I've got the seven best kiddos on the planet: a son and six daughters (Jolie, Rachel, Tina, QDIII, Kidada, Rashida, and Kenya), ranging in age from twenty-eight to seventy, and I'm grateful that God chose me to be their daddy. It's important to take a moment to reflect on all that we have, and sometimes, just bein' vertical is enough!

As I reflect on what turned out to be an almost fully international "Safer at Home" order in 2020, it has become even more clear that we don't have any control over what will happen tomorrow. But in the midst of it all, my hope and prayer is that our individual, creative voices may serve to share a glimpse of connectivity with those who need it most. And I pray that I will continue to do so even long after I'm gone.

Finally, as I wrote in the closing paragraph of my 2001 autobiography, "It is time to say that . . . the values you carry within yourself—of work, love, and integrity—carry the greatest worth, because these are what get you through with your dreams intact, your heart held firm, and your spirit ready for another day. Then, you can look back and say, I lived it 360 degrees, like my predecessors who cared and led me here, teaching me to approach

creativity with humility and respond to success with grace."
And now, nearly twenty years after writing that, I can attest to
the fact that it all still holds true. May we all recognize the value
of life, and live, love, and give as fiercely as we can, wherever
we can. Even twenty years later, these same values hold true.

It's an amazing journey, so enjoy every drop of it, and you
better believe that I'm going to bop until I drop!

The following blank pages are yours and it's up to you to do
what you want with it. Big-time love and props!

YOLO KOKO. You Only Live Once, So Keep On Keepin' On!

ACKNOWLEDGMENTS

Writing acknowledgments for a book is incredibly difficult, because the truth is, I want to thank *everyone* who's ever been a part of my life. However, it's impossible to capture the gratitude I have for each and every person who has helped shape the man I am today. So, I will limit myself by only including those who have directly contributed to the completion of this specific book. As for the rest of y'awl, you know who you are! Big, BIG-time love and props.

Abel "The Weeknd" Tesfaye

Adam Fell

Adam Hart

Alex Banayan

Alyssa Lein Smith

Annalea Manalili

Armando Abate

Arnold Robinson

Ben Fong-Torres

Brittany Palmer

Chris Sinada

Christiana Wilkinson

Clare Mao

Debborah Foreman

Diane Shaw

Don Passman

Edgar Macias

Erik Hyman

Fabiola Martinez

Gavin Wise

Gezelle Rodil

Glenn Fuentes

Gloria Echenique

Greg Gorman

Gregg Ramer

James Cannon

Jeff Cannon

Jenice Kim

Jeremy Barrett

Jessica Wiener

John Cannon

Jordan Abrams

Kathy Cannon

Leah Petrakis

Mamie VanLangen

Marc Gerald

Maria Bonilla	Rebecca Kaplan
Max Mason	Richard Jones
Melissa Mahood	Roger Trujillo
Michael Davis	Rory Anderson
Michael LaTorre	Ruth Chee
Michael Peha	Sal Slaiby
Natasha Martin	Sarah Masterson Hally
Nikita Lamba	Stacy Creamer
Patrick Jordan	Teresa Bojorquez
Paul Aguilar	Tess Callero
Ramona Fabie	Thomas Duport

And of course, my BELOVED children and grandchildren, without whom I am nothing!: Jolie, Rachel, Tina, QDIII, Kidada, Rashida, Kenya, Donovan, Sunny, Eric, Jessica, Renzo, Linnea, Isaiah, Tesla, and Billy Basie.

**In loving memory of my dearly
beloved sisters-in-law
Gloria "GG" Jones and Jacquie Avant**